Cambridge Elements

Elements of Sustainability: Science, Policy, Practice
Series Editor-in-Chief
Arun Agrawal
University of Michigan

HOW TO NORMATIVELY TRANSFORM FOOD SYSTEMS

Propositions of a Holistic Framework of Politics

Abdul-Rahim Abdulai
Alliance of Bioversity and the International Center for Tropical Agriculture

Christophe Béné
Alliance of Bioversity and the International Center for Tropical Agriculture

Shaftesbury Road, Cambridge CB2 8EA, United Kingdom

One Liberty Plaza, 20th Floor, New York, NY 10006, USA

477 Williamstown Road, Port Melbourne, VIC 3207, Australia

314–321, 3rd Floor, Plot 3, Splendor Forum, Jasola District Centre, New Delhi – 110025, India

103 Penang Road, #05–06/07, Visioncrest Commercial, Singapore 238467

Cambridge University Press is part of Cambridge University Press & Assessment, a department of the University of Cambridge.

We share the University's mission to contribute to society through the pursuit of education, learning and research at the highest international levels of excellence.

www.cambridge.org
Information on this title: www.cambridge.org/9781009509640
DOI: 10.1017/9781009509633

© Abdul-Rahim Abdulai and Christophe Béné 2025

This publication is in copyright. Subject to statutory exception and to the provisions of relevant collective licensing agreements, no reproduction of any part may take place without the written permission of Cambridge University Press & Assessment.

When citing this work, please include a reference to the DOI 10.1017/9781009509633

First published 2025

A catalogue record for this publication is available from the British Library

ISBN 978-1-009-50964-0 Hardback
ISBN 978-1-009-50961-9 Paperback
ISSN 2635-0211 (online)
ISSN 2635-0203 (print)

Cambridge University Press & Assessment has no responsibility for the persistence or accuracy of URLs for external or third-party internet websites referred to in this publication and does not guarantee that any content on such websites is, or will remain, accurate or appropriate.

For EU product safety concerns, contact us at Calle de José Abascal, 56, 1°, 28003 Madrid, Spain, or email eugpsr@cambridge.org

How To Normatively Transform Food Systems

Propositions of a Holistic Framework of Politics

Elements of Sustainability: Science, Policy, Practice

DOI: 10.1017/9781009509633
First published online: August 2025

Abdul-Rahim Abdulai
Alliance of Bioversity and the International Center for Tropical Agriculture

Christophe Béné
Alliance of Bioversity and the International Center for Tropical Agriculture

Author for correspondence: Abdul-Rahim Abdulai, a.abdulai@cgiar.org

Abstract: This Element draws from an extensive literature review on food politics to propose a Framework of Holistic Politics for Food System Transformation. The Framework posits that food systems transformation would be a process/outcome of interrelated political configurations of actions across four processes or stages: (1) identifying resistance to change in the current regime; (2) creating and sustaining new momentum; (3) converting new momentum into sustainable options – and cross-cutting; (4) managing trade-offs, reducing incoherence, and prioritization. At each stage, four domains of politics must be considered, including: (1) power, the political economy of actors, knowledge, and evidence; (2) cultural dynamics, norms, and behavior; (3) capacity and financial resources; and (4) technological innovations). To deliver normative transformation, these actions must be carried out in four distinct processes. The Framework underscores the need for normative and goal-oriented processes, the multidimensionality of politics, and the normative driving environment in governance food systems transformation.

Keywords: food systems transformation, food system governance, transformation, politics, political economy, enabling environment

© Abdul-Rahim Abdulai and Christophe Béné 2025

ISBNs: 9781009509640 (HB), 9781009509619 (PB), 9781009509633 (OC)
ISSNs: 2635-0211 (online), 2635-0203 (print)

Contents

1	Introduction	1
2	The Foundational Frameworks	4
3	A Holistic Framework of Politics for Food Systems Transformation	7
4	The Political (In)actions within Domains and Processes of Food Systems Transformation	17
5	Delivering Normative Food Systems Transformation through Politics – What the Framework Teaches Us	76
6	Concluding Reflections	84
	References	92

1 Introduction

Food systems transformation – increasingly understood as purposive and drastic changes that improve food systems processes and outcomes (Béné, 2022) – has undoubtedly become a buzzword in "food" literature, policy, and within global development communities. This attention is partly due to persistent challenges and failures of the current food system; over 828 million people were facing hunger, and 3.1 billion people were without affordable healthy diets in 2021. Food systems accounted for over 32% of the global disease burden (Imran & Imran, 2020; World Health Organization, 2020) and 21%–37% of the global GHG emissions around the same period (FAO, 2022; FAO et al., 2021). Scholars have, therefore, acknowledged the urgency of the food system transformation (Fanzo & Davis, 2021; Webb et al., 2020; Willett et al., 2019). For example, the 2021 United Nations Food System Summit (UNFSS) followed up on some high-profile expert reports such as EAT-Lancet (Willett et al., 2019), the International Panel of Experts on Sustainable Food Systems (IPES-Food, 2016), and the High-Level Panel of Experts on Food Security and Nutrition (HLPE, 2019) to emphasize the global need to redirect what scholars have described as broken, dysfunctional and unsustainable food system (Baker et al., 2021; Fanzo et al., 2021; Lartey et al., 2018; Marsden et al., 2018; Okoro Godwin Elechi et al., 2022a; Oliver et al., 2018; Ruben et al., 2021) toward alternatives that deliver resilience, equity, health, and sustainable outcomes (Conti et al., 2021; Fanzo et al., 2021; Webb et al., 2020). Essentially, there is a renewed mobilization of actors and political interest to transform food systems.

Markedly, a corollary of the drive for transformations is the enhanced attention and visibility of the issue, partly evident in actors' cogitation on purposively guiding the process. From specific actions (e.g., Okoro et al., 2022) to policies (bundles) (e.g., Barrett et al., 2022), and pathways (e.g., Dentoni et al., 2017), as well as paradigm shifts (e.g., Ruben et al., 2021; Sandhu, 2021), scholars are scrambling for potential solutions. Specifically, from specific proposals to reduce meat intake (Rust et al., 2020; Willett et al., 2019) to the structural reconstitution of governance arrangements (Fraser et al., 2016; Garnett, 2013), we are experiencing an enormous charge to redirect food systems. These propositions are expansive and diverse, and we do not intend for an exhaustive stock here. Instead, we observe and posit that these proposals collectively express restructuring of how actions, decision-making, and relationships in the current food systems are constituted and performed (De Schutter, 2017; Ruben et al., 2021). The breadth and diversity of proposals, we note, foreshadow the inevitable need for negotiation in respect of competing and potentially conflicting "means to the desired end" (Conti et al., 2021;

Duncan et al., 2022; Ingram, 2011; Jagustovic et al., 2021; Juri et al., 2022; Oliver et al., 2018; van Bers et al., 2019). Simply put, transforming food systems involves politics (Anderson & Leach, 2019; Baker et al., 2021; Béné, 2022).

By politics, we refer to Barry's (2002, p. 270) description of the "political" as an "index of the space of disagreement" and "politics" as "a set of technical practices, forms of knowledge and institutions." Politics, viewed as the political, deals with the struggles and negotiations between classes, interests, and movements. But politics also entails dealing with the anti-political, which Barry (2002) described as resistance processes that seek to restrain the political, and Braun (2015, p. 1) remarks that resistance serves as "strategic containment of potentially more radical futures." Politics is, therefore, the arena and processes where we deal with the tensions of the political – the disagreements – and the anti-political – resistance seeking to maintain the status quo (Carolan, 2020). In this Element, we describe politics as the management of contestations, resistance, and making choices to steer food systems activities and processes toward normative outcomes. It involves struggles between actors, interests, processes, goals, and values and the dialogues of what and how to do them.

Discussions of politics have gained prominence in the food system transformation literature (see, for example, Anderson et al., 2019; Anderson & Leach, 2019; Hassanein, 2003; Leach et al., 2020; Sodano & Gorgitano, 2022; Swinburn, 2019). The crust of this scholarship is that disagreements and competitions – over facts, interests, values, and desired outcomes – are inherent in the food systems' transformations (Anderson et al., 2019). As Pelling (2010) puts it, actual change cannot occur without contention of the underlying social, political, and economic arrangements that have fashioned and maintained the existing status quo. In this case, we must embrace and tackle politics as avenues to unpack how transformations (may) occur or not (De Schutter, 2017; Leach et al., 2020; Leeuwis et al., 2021).

However, the nascent literature remains disordered, fragmented, and underdeveloped (Béné, 2022; Oliver et al., 2018), hindering the potency to offer clear guidance on how politics can be improved/leveraged for food system transformation. In essence, despite the calls to improve political processes for the prospects of positive outcomes (De Schutter, 2017; Gillespie et al., 2013; Oliver et al., 2018), there is little guidance on steps to follow, that is, *how to do so* (Béné, 2022). In fact, *how can food systems politics be improved and/or leveraged to deliver normative transformation?* Aware of this critical question, this Element proposes a holistic framework that will structure the disorderliness in the literature on the politics of food systems change to provide coherent direction on delivering the preferred transformation.

To build this holistic framework, we draw on two established frames – the Multi-level Perspectives of transition (MLP) (Geels, 2002; Geels & Schot, 2007) and the Framework for the creation of an Enabling Environment for Accelerated Undernutrition Reduction (henceforth FEEU) (Gillespie et al., 2013) (see next section) – that explain the dynamics of (food) systems change. We complement them with a non-exhaustive, but extensive, discussion of political actions from the literature that have been and can be used to transform food systems (Leach et al., 2020). We approach the review from a holistic perspective, drawing on transformation-relevant processes rooted in the traditional political economy analysis of structural issues and power dynamics (IPES-Food, 2017), complemented by more sociological locations of politics/power as embedded in discursive narratives (Keeley & Scoones, 2000), technological innovations (Hutter & Lawrence, 2021), knowledge (Szanton, 2004), and consumption activities (Boström & Micheletti, 2019). The outcome is a two-dimensional framework (of domains of politics and processes of transformation) that outlines how temporal configurations of political actions could be leveraged over four distinct phases to overcome persistent unsustainable regime trajectories and drive food systems toward normative transformative goals.

In what follows, we start by reviewing the two foundational frameworks to highlight their value and drawbacks, for which a new framework becomes imperative. Following that section, we introduce the Framework of Holistic Politics of Food Systems Transformation (the Framework here forth). In this framework, we posit that, for transformation to occur, actions are necessary across four domains of politics: (1) Political economy of actors, knowledge, and evidence; (2) Cultural dynamics, norms, and behavior; (3) Capacity and financial resources (of the public sector); and (4) Technological innovation. These actions must be carried out across four distinct phases and processes of transformation: (1) Identifying resistance to change in the current regime; (2) Creating and sustaining new momentum; (3) Converting new momentum into sustainable options – and a cross-cutting, (4) Managing trade-offs, reducing incoherence, and prioritizing actions. To put the proposed Framework in context, we document and discuss practiced and proposed political actions across the different domains that could be applied at each stage to steer food system transformation. Ultimately, the exercise provides the missing, yet much-needed, guidance that shepherds the fragmented political actions into a coherent framework that could guide how actors can enact normative food systems transformation.

In the discussion, we reflect on three critical contributions and lessons from the framework. First, we discuss the need for normativity and goal orientation in the food system transformation process. For goal orientation, we note that the framework extends the frontiers of transformation actions by intentionally avoiding path dependency, pursuing multiple dimensions of change, and aligning with sustainability goals. Second, we emphasize the multidimensionality of food system transformation made evident through the framework, arguing for change actions to move beyond technological solutions to cater to the political economy of actors, capacities, resources, cultural norms, and consumer behaviors. Third, through the different roles of different actors and their politics discussed at various stages of the framework, we reflect on how the politics of food systems could create a driving environment for the transformation of the governance needed for the great food transformations to happen.

We conclude this Element with cautious optimism, calling on policy decision-makers and all relevant food system actors to consider this as a guide to unlock lock-ins and drive food systems toward sustainable trajectories. We also call for contextual adaptability to consider the unique politics dictated by differences in political circumstances, food system types, and dynamics (e.g., traditional vs consolidated). The conclusion also entreats researchers and practitioners to continue enhancing the framework by injecting and complementing it with practical experiences, contexts, and subject-based theories.

Ultimately, this Element brings diverse politics into a holistic framework that policy and decision actors could contextually leverage to diagnose food systems' resistances and normatively guide food systems' transformation. In the process, this Element makes significant contributions to food system transformation efforts and literature by highlighting and centering diverse politics within the broader frame of how to achieve the Great Food Transformation.

2 The Foundational Frameworks

First, we draw from the MLP, a hybrid analytical framework between evolutionary approaches and interpretivism that theorizes and explains patterns of long-term change in socio-technical systems (Geels, 2002; Rip & Kemp, 1998). The MLP, which aims to explain how (technological) transitions come about, takes a systems-based approach to understanding and analyzing large-scale, socio-technical transitions (El Bilali, 2020; Geels, 2019). It conceptualizes socio-technical transitions as "non-linear processes that result from the interplay of developments at three analytical levels: niches (the locus for radical innovations and alternatives), dominant regimes (the locus of established practices and associated rules that stabilize existing systems), and an exogenous landscape" (Geels, 2011, p. 27).

There are four critical processes in the MLP transition mechanism: (1) novel alternatives are created in the niches, which may take the form of new technologies, practices, configurations of actor groups, beliefs, values, networks, or policies (Darnhofer, 2015). (2) Niche innovations gain momentum through learning and performance to draw support from influential actor groups. (3) At the landscape level, pressures trickle down to the existing regime, destabilizing its business-as-usual practices to create windows of opportunity for novel innovations to penetrate. (4) The destabilization creates new alignments that allow a breakthrough of novelties into the regime (Geels, 2010; Geels & Schot, 2007). Transitions thus occur when there are shifts from one socio-technical regime to another (Hölscher et al., 2018). However, such shifts are mostly incremental and path-dependent because of lock-in mechanisms that seek to maintain old regimes, which scholars have repeatedly shown are driven by power structures and vested interests of incumbent actors (Avelino & Wittmayer, 2016; Conti et al., 2021).

The MLP has garnered significant and mixed interests in a variety of scholarly fields (see Lachman, 2013) – especially in energy and transport systems (Araújo, 2014; Bergh & Bruinsma, 2008; Geels, 2012) – as a heuristic to describe and guide sustainability transitions. A systematic review by El Bilali (2019) also found it the dominant framework used among agri-food scholars to explain food systems sustainability transitions (see also El Bilali, 2020). Nonetheless, some scholars (e.g., El Bilali, 2019) are unconvinced of its utility for transformation in the agri-food sector, and many other criticisms and responses are widely documented (Geels, 2011; Genus & Coles, 2008; Lawhon & Murphy, 2012). We do not wish to revisit these discussions but add our voices. First, while we appreciate the valuable insights MLP provides for food scholarship and practice (Hinrichs, 2014), we are unconvinced that a framework developed for other sectors can fully capture the unique complexities of the food systems (HLPE, 2017), such as the very disaggregated sources of food production and consumption practices. Second, the randomness rather than normativity of incremental transitions stipulated by the MLP may not be a capable fit for engendering the radical, urgent, goal-directed transformation that the unprecedented challenges of food systems require. These unique dynamics in agri-food systems and the need for a normativity of change (Béné, 2022) motivate us to enrich MLP thinking with food system politics to cater to the sector's specific needs.

Hence, we complement the MLP with the FEEU, which focuses on the governance of change through an enabling environment. Contrary to the theory-heaviness of the MLP, FEEU is a practice-informed framework developed from the experiences of practitioners working to reduce undernutrition worldwide

(Gillespie et al., 2013). It stipulates that an enabling environment, defined as "policy and policy processes that build and sustain momentum for the effective implementation of actions that reduce undernutrition" (p. 553), is critical for undernutrition reduction. An enabling environment for undernutrition reduction, according to FEEU, can be fashioned through political actions embedded in three linked factors (i.e., 1. knowledge and evidence, 2. politics and governance, and 3. capacity and resources) across two stages: (i.e., 1. the creation and sustaining of momentum; and 2. the conversion of the momentum into results). Unlike the MLP, FEEU suggests that calculated political processes at the intersections of broad economic, political, environmental, social, and cultural contexts can deliver the normative goal of reduced undernutrition (Smith & Haddad, 2015). Hence, it centers politics and deliberate actions of actors as the central elements to enacting desired societal change. Though FEEU focuses on undernutrition, it is believed to have broader applicability for other food systems goals, such as obesity reduction (Gillespie et al., 2013). Hence, researchers have drawn on its framing of an enabling environment to foreground undernutrition reduction and other nutrition goals (see Gillespie et al., 2015; Hunter et al., 2016; Smith & Haddad, 2015). What is evident in the later engagements with FEEU is that it does hold some prospects to positively influence nutrition outcomes and, possibly, other food system goals if practicalized.

However, FEEU, like any other framework, has limitations. Nisbet et al. (2014) acknowledged that the FEEU does not effectively consider how critical issues such as power, social accountability, and the role of political narrative affect enabling environments (Nisbett et al., 2014). Meanwhile, understanding these issues would be critical in dictating food systems' structures and processes (McNeill, 2019; Swinburn, 2019). Likewise, the FEEU does not explicitly cater to inevitable political issues that may resist changes, as well as the management of inevitable trade-offs in creating enabling environments for attaining desired food system outcomes. Essentially, despite the current practical relevance of the FEEU (Hunter et al., 2016), it would benefit from an extension with other aspects of politics. Beyond the need for such extensions, we are also uncertain whether a framework with nutrition as the underlying core purpose would be adequate to tackle the transformation of the whole food system(s) and deliver the multiple, sometimes conflicting outcomes. Meeting the ambitious goal(s) and the urgency of transforming food systems would require a more targeted framework that caters to the many politics that constitute and shape its dynamics.

In essence, the MLP and FEEU have merits and potential applicability for food systems change. However, they, singularly and jointly, still must be improved to enhance the prospects of adequately guiding food system transformation. Against this background, we adapt some relevant insights – including the temporary and processual dimensions of change in the MLP, the pluralistic politics of FEEU, and the roles and interactions of diverse actors at different stages in both frameworks – to propose a holistic framework for food systems transformation.

3 A Holistic Framework of Politics for Food Systems Transformation

Table 1 presents the holistic framework of politics proposed to steer normative food systems transformation. Before introducing the framework, we will note that using the word *holistic* is intentional as we consider the food systems transformation achievable through a systemic approach to change. The Framework thus combines the different politics and areas of food systems actions discussed in the literature to set out the steps for delivering food systems transformation. The Framework is organized into two axes: the vertical as *domains of politics* and the horizontal as *transformation processes/phases* (see Tables 1 and 2).

3.1 The Domains of Food System Politics

The domains of food systems politics describe the spaces of (a)political activities within which actions of resistance and mechanisms that break barriers and propel systematic change manifest. These domains are informed by the pluralistic and multidimensionality of politics identified in traditional political economy scholarships and related fields that take an interest in disagreements and negotiation of change actions (Anderson et al., 2019; Leach et al., 2020). We identify and propose two domains (1. Discursive practices / instrumental power and 2. Institutional capacity and technology) and four subdomains where anti(political) processes (must) define food systems dynamics. Being non-exhaustive, we briefly describe, in no order of significance, the political nature of each subdomain as they relate to food system transformations.

3.1.1 Domain A – Political Economy of Actors and Evidence

This domain describes how food systems change or stability is dependent on the political negotiation and struggles between actors (and their interests and values) (Harris et al., 2019), the interplay of socially and politically positioned knowledge (Sodano & Gorgitano, 2022; Tomlinson, 2013), and structurally determined rules of the game (Clapp, 2020). The domain is mainly established within political economy scholarship, where food systems dynamics are conceived to emanate from power dynamics embedded in structural, economic, institutional, and discursive forces (Anderson & Leach, 2019; Clark et al., 2021;

Table 1 Framework of holistic politics for food systems transformation

The processes		Issues and challenges in:		
The domains		1. Identifying resistance to change in the current regime	2. Creating and maintaining new momentum	3. Converting new momentum into sustainable options
Discursive practices / instrumental power	Framing, political economy of actors, knowledge, and evidence			
	Cultural dynamics, norms, and behaviors			
Institutional capacity and technology	Capacity and financial resources (of the public sector)			
	Technological innovation			
		4. Managing trade-offs, reducing incoherence, and prioritizing actions		

Table 2 The different political domains and processes involved in food system transformation

The domains	Domains of politics involved
A. Powers, discourses and knowledge	Powers, discourses and knowledge represent the different forms of direct control or influence of actors and the mechanisms through which those are channelled. Power in food systems is mainly established within political economy scholarship, where it is said to emanate from dynamics embedded in instrumental, structural, and discursive forces. It offers valuable insights into how existing deeply embedded unsustainable structures, institutions, discourses and knowledge, dominate and lock-in the system into its current trajectory but also how to leverage deep-rooted power dynamics to trigger transformations.
B. Culture, social norms and behaviors	Food choices and behaviors describe why and how individuals eat the foods they do. Food choices and behaviors, influenced by cultures and social norms, can slow down social change or, on the contrary, provide leverage for personal and collective reforms. Politics in this domain is understood in the context of socio-cultural struggles around change processes at individual and social/collective scales, as illustrated through, e.g., political consumerisms. Issues of culture and norms, however, are still under-represented in the literature on food systems or even rarely viewed as political.
C. Capacity and financial resources	Capacity and financial resources refer to the available human, organizational and financial assets available to institutions that facilitate food system actions. These resources have often been recognized as potentially highly political, for example, in the case of capacities and resources inadequacies in low- and middle-income countries' public administrations, leading to competition between public needs and priorities or between levels of public policy (national vs. sub-national), or between relevant sectors (e.g., health vs. education vs. agriculture).

Table 2 (cont.)

The domains	Domains of politics involved
D. Technological innovation	Technological innovation describes novel and better technologies, tools, systems, and technical processes in the food system space. It often viewed as engine of change, unavoidably implies competition between the new and the old, propelling particular values at the expense of others, and ultimately resulting in the reshaping of power relations in food systems. Through these and other mechanisms (e.g., lobbying), technological innovation is said to have the potential to catalyze transformations, while it is also very often source of inertia – making it a critical element to control in order to navigate transformations.

The processes	Nature of the processes involved
1. Identifying resistance to change in the current regime	The first process necessary in transforming food systems is identifying the resistance to change in the current food regime. Scholarships in political economy, socio-technical transitions, and innovation theories have all highlighted resistance as an integral element of food systems and the analysis of their dynamics. The argument is that dominant incumbents and established institutions may have interests in maintaining and protecting the structures on which their current position and benefits depend.
2. Creating and maintaining new momentum	After identifying and challenging resistances, the second process that needs to take place is creating and maintaining a new momentum, that is, the emergence of a new pathway (in the form of an alternative narrative, change in norms, behaviors, and/or institutional arrangements) that bears a different vision from the established regime/model/paradigm. This is the stage where the foundation for the normativity that must guide the transformation toward sustainable goals are made explicit.

Table 2 (cont.)

The processes	Nature of the processes involved
3. Converting new momentum into sustainable options	The third process consists in converting the new momentum into sustainable options. This stage refers to the step where the desirable emerging alternative momentum becomes mainstream to compete and replace the dominant unsustainable practices and structures. It is thus at this stage that alternative framings, technologies, behaviors and norms, and capacity arrangements created in the prior stage become institutionalized, converting new momentum into diffusible and followable prospects and new social, technological, economic and political standards.
4. Managing trade-offs, reducing incoherence, and prioritizing actions	Finally, crosscutting the three processes above is managing trade-offs, reducing incoherence, and prioritizing actions. Drawing from (food) systems perspective, we describe this stage as systematically assessing actions and policies to minimize contradictions and maximize co-benefits in processes and outcomes. Empirical data indicate that the many complexities of food systems – including competing issues, objectives, goals, and potential outcomes – make those trade-offs and prioritization critical to transformation processes since, ultimately, every action (as well-intentioned as it may be) always results in winners and losers.

Reproduced from Bene and Abdulai (2023)

De Schutter, 2017; Duncan et al., 2019; Harris et al., 2019). As probably the domain with the active scholarly engagements of food politics and power (Harris et al., 2019), it offers valuable insights into how deeply embedded unsustainable structures have come to dominate and lock-in and how to influence deep-rooted power dynamics to facilitate change actions.

3.1.2 Domain B – Cultural Dynamics, Norms, and Behaviors

This domain describes how food behaviors, as influenced by cultures and social norms (Higgs, 2015), are spaces of politics. The politics is evident in the conflicting abilities of how cultural norms strain social change or provide leverage for personal and collective reforms. According to Béné et al. (2020, p. 458), expected food "systems changes may conflict with, or diverge substantially from current or even still-to-emerge socio-cultural norms." In this sense, the politics in this domain is understood in the context of sociocultural struggles in change processes at individual and social scales. Discussions of values and meanings of food actions in social practices (e.g., Sargent, 2014; Shove et al., 2012; Spaargaren et al., 2011), and, increasingly, in poststructuralist-informed political economy (Duncan et al., 2019) through such works on political consumerisms (Goodman & DuPuis, 2002; Jacobsen & Dulsrud, 2007; Lockie, 2002) make these politics evident. However, issues of culture and norms, as Noack and Pouw (2015) argued, are still underrepresented in the food systems change and, even when included, are rarely viewed as political. This makes this domain imperative to extending the horizons and levers of politics of food systems transformations.

3.1.3 Domain C – Capacity and Financial Resources (of the Public Sector)

This domain describes how a limited resource base for enacting change breeds competition and conflicts among actors, activities, and pursued outcomes. Scholars in development, public administration, governance (Wu et al., 2015; Yee & Liu, 2021), and political economy (Gillespie et al., 2013) bring forth some of the politics in this domain. The discussions of public capacities and resource inadequacies, especially in LMIC, implicate the politics of resource use as they breed disagreements and competition (see Gillespie et al., 2013). Specifically, different public needs and priorities (e.g., food vs. transport) and levels of public actors (e.g., national and subnational – Pereira & Drimie, 2016), as well as various food systems priorities (e.g., health vs. education vs. agriculture) compete for limited capacities and finances. The political dynamics in this domain, thus, essentially translate into how the different mixes of competencies (analytical, operational, and political skills) and capabilities – or lack thereof (resources at individual, organizational, and systemic levels) – enable establishment/initiation of change/shifts, in practices and in mental models/paradigms of different governance, such as mechanisms of formulating and administering policies to counter resistance and deliver desired food systems outcomes (Gillespie et al., 2013).

3.1.4 Domain D – Technological Innovations

This domain describes how technological innovations conduits of (food) systems change (Bear & Holloway, 2015; Khan et al., 2021), imbue competition, conflicts, and tensions between the new and the old, as well as between the multiple innovations vying for attention (Herrero et al., 2020). Technologies cannot be detached from what they do (Carolan, 2020, p. 209) and how they come into being – which are mainly political. Thus, specific values are propelled at the expense of others in technological processes, ultimately resulting in the reshaping of power relations in food systems (Carolan, 2018a; ETC Group, 2022). Through these and other mechanisms, technological innovations are said to be ambiguous (Herrero et al., 2020), where, on the one hand, they may catalyze transformations (e.g., hybrid seeds and green revolution), and on the other hand, be a source of inertia (e.g., farmer capital investment in machinery limiting diversified production or defensive research and development – ERF, 2008). In this context, technological innovations are critical political spaces in navigating transformations.

The domains emphasize the multiple dimensions of food systems politics that must be considered in transformation processes (Duncan et al., 2019; Leach et al., 2020). Based on these diverse spaces of food politics and the following reviews, we postulate that food systems transformation would entail deliberate actions across multiple domains. Importantly, complexities in these domains mean one-time measures would not suffice; instead, they must be intentional throughout the transformation trajectory, which we delineate as consisting of four distinct processes. Those are described next and summarized in Table 1.

3.2 The Processes of Transformation (and Political Actions)

From Table 1, we conceive food systems transformation as a process/outcome of four interrelated (anti)political actions. This section expands on each of these processes and explains why they are critical to transformation of food systems.

3.2.1 Process 1 – Identifying Resistance to Change in the Current Regime

We stipulate that the first process in transformation is *identifying the resistance to change in the current food regime.* Scholarships in the political economy (De Schutter, 2017), socio-technical transitions (Anderson et al., 2019; Geels, 2014; Vanloqueren & Baret, 2009), and innovation resistance theories (Friedman & Ormiston, 2022) have underscored resistance – the mechanism through which system dynamics restrains newness and change – as an integral element of food systems (Conti et al., 2021, see also Goldstein et al., 2023 for an extensive review across disciplines). Within these scholarships, it is assumed that the natural response to any system disturbance is status quo stability, that is, resistance to maintain the standard and prevent novelties (Leeuwis et al., 2021; Pelling et al., 2015). For food systems, dominant and powerful structures – of narratives, knowledge, infrastructures, cultures, institutions, and so on (De Schutter, 2019; Harris et al., 2019) – have a strong interest in maintaining the status quo – in this case, unsustainable conventional and corporate food regimes (IPES-Food, 2017, 2023).

The inevitability of resistance and the challenges they pose to food systems sustainability efforts make their identification, understanding, and eventual unlocking a critical first step to transformation. De Schutter (2019, p. 17) has noted that the first insight into any food system change is a diagnosis of the source of the dominant inertia (Hoek et al., 2021; Jagustovic et al., 2021; Juri et al., 2022). As is well known, plotting for change without understanding where we are – and, by extension, what has brought us to the current state – risks repeating old mistakes that only (un)intentionally entrench unsustainable trajectories (HLPE, 2020). Likewise, since resistance (can) renders regimes receptive to change and water down alternatives to make them unattractive, unfeasible, and ineffective for reform purposes (Hübel & Schaltegger, 2022). Thus, alternatives would remain largely theoretical unless we identify and tackle the strong mechanisms that uphold food systems in their current undesirable state (Calo et al., 2021; Hübel & Schaltegger, 2022; Oliver et al., 2018). Essentially, challenging the status quo to overcome change-resisting biases is a prerequisite for transformation (Carriedo et al., 2022; Duncan et al., 2022; Fanzo et al., 2020), which makes understanding the mechanisms for dominance and persistence critical.

3.2.2 Process 2 – Creating and Maintaining New Momentum

We propose *creating and* maintaining *new momentum* as the second process in food system transformation. We view momentum as the emergence of new and alternative power forces with the potential to challenge and impact existing regimes in ways that sow the seeds for transformation. Drawing from socio-technical transitions (Bremmer & Bos, 2017; Geels, 2002) and alternative food networks (Tregear, 2011), these power forces could be alternative narratives, innovations, norms and behaviors, and institutional arrangements that bear politically different visions from the established regime/model/paradigm. Particularly, this stage is motivated by well-established concepts and processes of transitions/transformation, such as niches in the MLP (Bremmer & Bos, 2017; Schot & Geels, 2007) and the preparation phase of change described by Olsson et al. (2014) and Pereira et al. (2020). However, unlike niches that are novelties from lower levels and sheltered from the rigors of regime competition (Schot & Geels, 2007, 2008), new momentum takes a systematic, diffuse, and fluid approach as we envision these alternative forces to manifest across all domains and scales of food systems.

The importance of creating and maintaining new momentum cannot be overstated. Critical in new momentum is planting alternative visions and setting out a different direction for food systems (Lam et al., 2022). At this stage, alternative visions, directions, and expectations that will drive the trajectory of the food systems transformation are articulated and deliberately crafted into change actions, innovations, narratives, processes, and practices (Jia, 2021; Kugelberg et al., 2021; Lartey et al., 2018). It sets the foundation for the explicit normativity actors must pursue to deliver alternative outcomes. It is where the actual goals of transformation, for example, sustainable healthy diets, are fused into the emerging food systems by employing such visions as the indices for negotiating political actions and setting up activities of change. As a stage of visioning, it also provides the avenue for creating and showcasing alternatives as a first step to challenging the status quo and delivering desirable change that cannot be achieved with the norm.

3.2.3 Process 3 – Converting New Momentum into Sustainable Options

The third process in transformation is *converting new momentum into sustainable options*. Taking inspiration from niche-regime linkages in MLP (Bui et al., 2016; Ingram, 2015; Lam et al., 2022), diffusion/adoption of innovations (Rogers, 1983), and the recruitment of practitioners in social practices (Shove & Pantzar, 2005; Shove et al., 2012), we describe this stage as the process of enlarging, replicating, and moving alternative forces and actions (Prost, 2019) into available political opportunities for others to follow its "*dance language*"[1] (Grüter & Farina, 2009). Hence, similar to the H3 in the three-horizon model (see Sharpe et al., 2016), the desirable alternative emerging futures of food systems politics (framings, technologies, behaviors and norms) become mainstream to become institutionalized as sustainable options from which potential takers can choose.

Converting momentum into sustainable options is of utmost importance in the transformation process. The availability of alternative or motivation alone is not enough to make niches become the norm, in this case, to turn alternatives into sustainable regime options. A prerequisite for transformation is thus drawing the right external partners or followers for new alternatives to become the standard (Aramyan et al., 2021). Likewise, developing alternatives into sustainable options within the regime offers prospects for including a diversity of

---

[1] Dance language is used in reference to the waggle dance made by bees to direct others to sources of nectar.

actors as people follow them, which can minimize the risk of negative transformation (Ferraboschi et al., 2022; Schoneveld, 2022). Finally, "selling new ideas and visions" to diverse actors as available options will provide a legitimacy test for potential futures. Since alternative visions and outcomes must be acceptable to potential takers (Shove & Pantzar, 2005; Shove & Walker, 2014) to draw transformation-worthy engagements, this stage is an opportunity to gauge how well actors may receive regime-altering politics.

3.2.4 Process 4 – Managing Trade-offs, Reducing Incoherence, and Prioritizing Actions

Finally, cross-cutting the three processes of transformation outlined so far is a critical process of *managing trade-offs, reducing incoherence, and prioritizing actions*. Trade-offs in this context refer to how an improvement in the status of one aspect of the food system or the choice to undertake one action is necessarily associated with a decline or loss of a different aspect (cf IPBES, 2017). We draw from (food) systems perspectives (Horton et al., 2017; Mausch et al., 2020) to describe this stage as systematically assessing actions to minimize contradictions and maximize co-benefits in processes and outcomes (HLPE, 2017; Jagustovic et al., 2021; Vågsholm et al., 2020). The goal is employing appropriate tools and processes to ensure that desirable change in one goal also contributes (in)directly toward other goals (synergies) while reaching one goal does not undermine or limit the potential of reaching another goal in the short- or long-term (trade-offs) (Jagustovic et al., 2021). Whether within the resistance to change or which alternative(s) yield maximum impacts with limited resources, trade-offs are fundamental in every food system in-action (Horton et al., 2017) and thus must be inherent at every stage of the transformation process.

The many complexities of food systems, including competing values (e.g., economics or environment) and potential outcomes (e.g., food security or environmental sustainability or resilience or equity), make trade-offs and prioritization critical to transformation processes. Ultimately, every in-action may result in winners and losers, which must be managed to ensure the least resistance possible. Thus, scholars have argued that trade-offs need to be intentionally addressed for true sustainability to occur (Elmqvist et al., 2013; Herrero et al., 2021; Zurek et al., 2021). Also, as Brouwer et al. (2021) note, inherent trade-offs and synergies across and within the different components of food systems (e.g., livestock farming, crop production, and fisheries) and between expected outcomes of behavior, such as diets that are healthy, sustainable, or affordable, call for intentional measures to ensure the attainment of one goal furthers others in the process to reduce conflicts and minimize losers while maximizing winners. Finally, management of trade-offs and prioritization essentially serves as a rate-limiting factor for change actions, which is desperately needed in the context of limited resources – of time, human capital, and finances – that are available to deliver desired food system outcomes (Gillespie et al., 2013).

4 The Political (In)actions within Domains and Processes of Food Systems Transformation

Having introduced the domains of politics and processes of food systems transformation – as the foundational components of the Framework – we turn our attention to the literature to identify and discuss specific political (in)actions and issues at the intersections of the domains and the processes in the context of the global food systems. In particular, we use interpretative analysis of the existing literature, clustering key themes, and authors' extensive practical experiences in the field to illustrate critical political issues, actions, and processes that can practically situate the Framework. While we have tried to cover the breadth of political actions at each stage, we acknowledge that some issues may have been missed in our analysis. Other actions discussed may also be open to inevitable contestations due to differences in interpretations and the diversity of pathways to transformation. Nonetheless, this exercise of populating the framework with propositions in literature partly illustrates its potential utility for understanding and guiding normative food system transformation. The rest of this section delves into the details of various political actions for transforming food systems at the intersection of the domains and processes of transformation.

4.1 Issues in Identifying Resistance to Change in the Current Regime

In line with the first process of the Framework, this section discusses various resistances to food systems transformation across the four domains. Given the critical position of resistance in transformation processes, scholars have identified and discussed many specific examples relative to global food systems (see Conti et al., 2021; Friedman & Ormiston, 2022; Goldstein et al., 2023; Oliver et al., 2018). We do not wish to take stock of these resistances – as other extensive reviews exist (e.g. Conti et al., 2021; Even et al., 2024). We, however, draw on that rich literature to illustrate how some identified barriers align with the Framework. Table 3 illustrates specific barriers and resistance to change in global food systems across the different domains of politics, and the following sections expand on these issues as discussed in the literature.

Table 3 Identifying resistance to change in the current regime

Domains	The process	1. Identifying resistance to change in the current regime	
		Issues	Selected references
Discursive practices / instrumental power	Framing, political economy of actors, knowledge, and evidence	• Concentration and domination by the "big corporate" • Current/dominant regime coalitions' discourses – Justification (narrative) of the current status quo • Lobbying, power of influence of incumbents (private sector) • Role of scientific paradigms and mainstream science • Economic and political interests from governments (e.g., trade export) • Dysfunctional policy-science interface and the role of media	(Baker et al., 2021; Béné, 2022; Conti et al., 2021; De Schutter, 2014; ETC Group, 2022; Friedman & Ormiston, 2022; Friel, 2021; IPES-Food, 2017, 2023; Moodie et al., 2021; Sievert et al., 2021)
	Cultural dynamics, norms, and behavior	• Users and consumer lifestyle and values • Habitus, norms, and societal expectations	(Azuike et al., 2011; Berger, 2019; Nyborg et al., 2016; Sargant, 2014; Spaargaren et al., 2011; Tan et al., 2016)

Institutional capacity and technology	Capacity and financial resources (of the public sector)	• Lack of human and/or capital resources in government institutions • Lack of know-how in government institutions	(Apampa et al., 2021; Babu, 2020; Gillespie et al., 2019; Pereira & Drimie, 2016; Sonnino et al., 2019; Yee & Liu, 2021; Zerbian et al., 2022)
	Technological innovation	• Technological path dependency and lock-in • Absence of alternative technological solution	(Aramyan et al., 2021; Conti et al., 2021; ETC Group, 2022; Friedman & Ormiston, 2022; Goldstein et al., 2023; Pignatti et al., 2015; Vanloqueren & Baret, 2009)

4.1.1 Resistance Related to the Political Economy of Actors, Knowledge, and Evidence

In this section, we discuss some resistance related to the political economy of actors, knowledge, and evidence described in the literature as hindering food systems transformation.

4.1.1.1 Concentration and Domination by the "Big Corporate."

Perhaps the most significant lock-in [in food systems-our emphasis] is political in nature: large actors opposing change because they are the beneficiaries of the current system have acquired a veto power allowing them to block reform, and it takes political courage to confront them (De Schutter, 2014, p. 233).

As succinctly captured by De Schutter (2014) and widely discussed by political economy scholars, the influence of powerful corporate actors is at the heart of opposition to food system reforms. "Big Food" and "Big Ag," as they are commonly called, are the super influential food businesses that wield enormous powers in their respective segments of the food system (Bronson & Sengers, 2022; Carolan, 2017; Stuckler & Nestle, 2012). However, drawing from Friedmann's (1982) reference to the possible emergence of corporate food regimes, we prefer "Big-Corporate" as an encompassing terminology to include the growing influences beyond the traditional Big Food. "Outsiders" such as technology companies (e.g., Microsoft and Google) and financial institutions have gained influence through digital innovations (Abdulai, 2022; Bronson & Sengers, 2022; ETC Group, 2022) and financialization and capitalization processes (Clapp, 2014), respectively, to exert control within food systems. Hence, "Big-Corporate" is a more appropriate description of the present situation.

Scholars argue that multiple – sometimes nefarious – (in)actions of corporations have tended to resist desired food systems reorganizations. At the core of considerable corporate resistance is the concentration of resources in a few hands (Clapp, 2021; ETC Group, 2022; IPES-Food, 2017). The politics here are in "the devil's name": by their very existence – in size, power, and resources – they dominate and wield considerable influence on activities, processes, and outcomes. For example, by 2022, only four firms controlled half of global commercial seeds, six companies controlled 58% of seed markets, six firms controlled 72% of the animal pharmaceutical market, four firms controlled 68% of the agrochemical market, and three companies controlled about 100% of commercial poultry genetics worldwide (ETC Group, 2022). Concentrations like these have also been documented in different food sectors, such as meat (e.g., Sievert et al., 2021), ultra-processed foods (e.g., Baker et al., 2020; Moodie et al., 2021), first foods (e.g., Baker et al., 2021) and retail (e.g.,

Hendrickson et al., 2020). Most of these are noted by scholars to have reached the economic threshold of "highly concentrated," where 60% of the market share is controlled by a few companies (Clapp, 2021). The processes leading to such concentrations are well discussed by scholars (see Clapp, 2021; ETC Group, 2022; Hendrickson et al., 2020; IPES-Food, 2017; Yates et al., 2021), so we would resist the temptation to repeat them here. But their role as resistance to change is of the essence.

Classical economists and business scholars generally view concentration positively for efficiencies (Bain, 1954; Gale & Branch, 1982), where, for example, they lead to economies of scale in production and avenues for sharing resources. However, experiences, including those in the agri-food system highlighted earlier, have challenged these interpretations; concentrations through mergers or any other forms of their metamorphization put resources in the hands of the few who use them to frustrate competitive innovations (Béné, 2022; Clapp, 2021). They consolidate power and influence over resources, finances, markets, research, and so on, making incumbents "too big" to challenge, compete against, or displace – thereby maintaining and protecting the status quo (IPES-Food, 2017). As Clapp (2021, p. 406) puts it, "The power at the disposal of concentrated firms and the strategies they pursue to influence the market, technology, and policy contexts overlap and reinforce each other in complex ways." The (non)deliberate (in)actions of big corporations under strong incentives to maintain the political and power status quo (Herrero et al., 2020, p. 267) tilt toward the anti-political as they leverage diverse strategies, including discourses.

4.1.1.2 Current/Dominant Regime Coalitions' Discourses and Justification (Narrative) of the Current Status Quo

A significant source of resistance in food systems today is how powerful regime actors shape and dominate discourses to justify the status quo and entrench their power and influence. Among other discursive strategies, Big Corporate players actively work to deflect attention from their power grabs by promoting a distorted picture of global food and agricultural systems (ETC Group, 2022). Other forms of domination of discourses include compartmentalized frames that diagnose food system problems in simplistic or reductionist forms or spinning false narratives (Anderson et al., 2019; ETC Group, 2022). The dominant framing of food systems futures championed by conventional big corporations and their supporters around the now de facto what Corolan (2017) described as *absent presents, a certain* 9 billion people desperately needing feeding by 2050, speaks to this challenge. For example, the "Produce More. Conserve More. Improve Farmers' Lives." campaign by Monsanto was built around the false narrative of a need to double production by 2050 (Peekhaus, 2010). By framing, rather uncritically and based on incorrect statistics, the future of food through an alarmist discourse on population growth, hunger, and climate change, powerful frames around the need to "feed the world" solidify a singular emphasis on productivity in favor of corporate-led technological advancements of the status quo (Tomlinson, 2013).

By drawing on the media through advertisement and disguised philanthropic influences on supranational bodies, such as the UN, FAO, and WHO – corporations permeate and implant their world views and agenda. References to a climate change and pandemic broken food system that require fixing in the lead-up to the UNFSS in 2021, for which they (big corporates) can partner as stakeholders, have come under scrutiny (Canfield et al., 2021a; Clapp et al., 2021). Such language deflected attention from the peasants' and smallholders' role in the future of food toward status quo reinforcing technocratic solutions and de-democratized food system transformations (Canfield et al., 2021a). By deploying terminologies like ecological modernization, climate-smart agriculture, and sustainable intensification, these tactics have come to obscure the broader social, cultural, political, and spatial dimensions of food and agriculture, which are at the heart of alternatives such as agroecology (Anderson et al., 2019; Holt-Giménez & Altieri, 2013). These are exacerbated by the spinning of narratives against such alternatives, as with the depoliticization of agroecology in the last decades – partly through trivializing it as backward and inefficient (Anderson et al., 2019). The battles between red meat and alternative meat and the framings of the problem as wicked problems, thereby engendering complex solutions, also exemplify how such discursive mechanisms resist change and perpetuate unsustainability (see Béné & Lundy, 2023 for an extended discussion).

Essentially, corporate entities deploy discourses to justify their activities as well as undermine the legitimacy of alternatives – both of which serve to resist desirable change (see also Drummond, 2013; Hinton, 2022). These discourse practices dilute and cast doubts about the way forward while legitimizing unsustainable activities. Whether these are intentional or otherwise is debatable as some, though primarily proponents of such actions, may view them as good faith efforts to support change. However, some evidence, including lobbying activities (see *4.1.1.3*), shows that these discourse dominations are more intentional rather than coincidental.

4.1.1.3 Lobbying, Power of Influence of Incumbents (Private Sector)

Lobbying activities of big corporations in food are well documented by researchers and organizations as a strategy for capturing policy, furthering status quo interests, and resisting/undermining alternatives (see Baker et al., 2020; Baker et al., 2021; IPES-Food, 2017; Moodie et al., 2021; Schoneveld, 2022). The case of failures of GMO labeling in the United States is of interest. Since 2015, it has been noted that food corporations spent at least $192.8 million to influence GMO labeling legislation, state-based referenda on GMO labeling laws, and other issues relating to consumer access to information. From January to June 2015 alone, Coca-Cola, PepsiCo, Kellogg's, Kraft Heinz Co., Land O'Lakes, and General Mills spent about 20 million in regulatory-killing lobbying[2] (IPES-Food, 2017). Furthermore, in 2014, Nestlé spent an estimated US$160,000 lobbying concerning the Special Supplemental Nutrition Program for Women, Infants, and Children (WIC) program, which provisions free formula for low-income families and for which companies "bid" to secure preferred provider status in state-level contracts, with bids often at or below cost (Tanrikulu et al., 2020). Corporations in seed and chemical sectors, ultra-processed food, and retail are noted to heavily feature in these practices (extensive discussion can be found in Baker et al., 2020; Baker et al., 2021; IPES-Food, 2017; Moodie et al., 2021; Schoneveld, 2022).

Lobbying practices in their varied forms are instrumental to frustrating transformations in food systems, especially when they prop up incumbent practices at the expense of potential alternatives. In documenting the growing influence and profits of ultra-processed food corporations, Moodie et al. (2021) argued that corporate lobbying puts profits over health to undermine the prevention of NCDs. Hence, they entrench unsustainable trajectories of profit-making status quo and prevent the emergence and growth of disruptive alternatives, such as potentially healthy diets, as in the case of the United States.

While lobbying is often associated with questionable intentions of corporate operations, the practice and its effects on food systems are much more complicated. Organizations, institutions, and industries use lobbying to influence legislation in their favor because it is not entirely wrong or illegal in most cases, as evident in most developed countries' open secret approach to it (Willis, 2015). Hence, even well-meaning entities sometimes lobby to bring forth favorable policies and draw attention to critical issues amid the competing demands for government attention. For example, the Community Food Coalition in the United States successfully lobbied for food reforms on many occasions (see 4.3.1.2). Hence, whether used by ill-intentioned corporations or well-meaning organizations seeking to protect the

---

[2] www.foxbusiness.com/features/kraft-pepsi-coke-others-want-to-keep-gmos-their-little-secret.

public interest, lobbying would likely remain an integral practice in the governance of food systems.

Thus far, we have provided a non-exhaustive discussion of how the actions of the big corporations dictate and frustrate transformation. While corporate activities, justifiable, have been under the research microscope, especially among political economy scholars (e.g., Anderson & Leach, 2019; Clapp, 2021), resistance to food systems is more profound and not an exclusivity of private actors.

4.1.1.4 Role of Scientific Paradigms and Mainstream Science

The current scientific paradigm is another source of food system inertia. Scholars have drawn attention to challenges in the current scientific paradigm and mainstream science, including poor funding mechanisms, bad incentives such as "publish or perish" in the academic environment, poor peer review processes, and rushed outputs (Tyfield et al., 2017). The consequences and sometimes the drivers of these challenges are the politicization of science, with mainstream regime actors such as the big corporates at the heart of such politics. Whether through lobbying or direct use of financial research capacity, corporate entities remain at the table of research agenda-setting despite the risk of conflict of interest and jeopardy of scientific integrity (Yates et al., 2021). For instance, in 2013, the combined R&D budgets of the Big Six agrochemical and seed companies, valued at $6.59 billion, was six times larger than the total USDA Agricultural Research and Information's $1.1 billion budget (USDA, 2013), and twenty times bigger than the CGIAR's $332.2 million expenditures on crop-oriented research/breeding in the same year (IPES-Food, 2017). With such research capacity comes the power to influence the direction of transformation through influencing facts, knowledge, and evidence (Anderson et al., 2019).

Baker et al. (2021) extensively discuss how the knowledge politics of Nestle brings this resistance into focus. With the world's largest private nutrition research capability, partly through the Nestle Nutrition Institute with over 5,000 staff in over 30 facilities across the world, they generate about 200 peer-reviewed articles each year. The company also indirectly influences the research agenda of supposed "independent actors" through the philanthropic arm, Nestle Foundation. Unsurprising, the majority of evidence produced through these activities barely questions, but instead justifies, industry interest and their products through biomedical and nutri-centric interpretation of, for example, infant and child nutrition from the lenses of fortification, reformulation, and development of novel product ingredients. Understandably, such evidence and knowledge cannot be fully trusted (Baker et al., 2021; Yates et al., 2021), to a large extent of considerable evidence of the negative consequences associated with promoted products, like the well-documented health impacts of baby formula (Ip et al., 2007; Krasny, 2012). Part of these politics is also cherry-picking and manipulating evidence to foster a favorable knowledge environment that entrenches and justifies their activities at the expense of legitimate science (see Béné, 2022).

By supporting and producing research that favors limited interests, big corporates and their supporters not only entrench their values in knowledge and policy but also foster an environment of polarization of ideas that slow down the transformation toward healthier and more sustainable foods (Béné, 2022; Nelson & Tallontire, 2014; Sievert et al., 2021). The result of this is a general lack of trust in science among the public, as evident in growing confusion around the actual impacts of certain food system actions, such as the consumption of red meat (Sievert et al., 2021) and climate change impacts of food behaviors (Almiron & Zoppeddu, 2015). Also critical to science-related resistance is how politics break trust at the interface of science and policy, as discussed in 4.1.1.6.

4.1.1.5 Economic and Political Interests from Governments (e.g., Trade Export)

Governments undoubtedly played crucial roles in past food system transformations, evident in state extension, research activities, and even input subsidies during the Green Revolution (Evenson, 2003; Jirström, 2005). These experiences naturally place greater expectations on them as probably the most critical actors expected to drive transformations using their extensive regulatory, legislative, and other powers to lay the foundation for the emergence and growth of sustainable alternatives (Gillespie et al., 2013; van Bers et al., 2019). However, governments, though expected to represent and protect the public interest, sometimes (in)deliberately contribute to resistance as they pursue their economic and political goals and those of their "generous" backers (see Bates, 2014; Renick, 2020). The financial interests and the political agenda of governments have become entangled with the dominant regime actors, and it is currently impossible for them to confidently pursue radical changes without undermining their own interests (Béné, 2022). These entanglements are tied to inputs of the corporate-facilitated unsustainable trajectories to the Gross Domestic Product (GDP), tax revenues, exports, and employment. In the United States, for example, agriculture, food, and related industries employed 22.1 million people (10.4% of total employment in 2022) and contributed roughly $1.537 trillion to US gross domestic product (GDP), a 5.5% share in 2023 (USDA, 2025).

These contributions mean governments not only turn a blind eye to unsustainable industry activities but actively support them through harmful incentives, such as subsidies, tax breaks, and grants, while simultaneously reducing positive incentives, such as research funding and social protection. For instance, despite growing sustainability concerns around red-meat, Tyson Foods in the United States, one of the world's largest meat processors, has received more than $316 million in state and local subsidies and $4 million in loans since 1989 (Subsidy Tracker, 2023). The result of these subsidies is production growth and persistence of red meat with no signs of slowing down: commercial red meat production in the United States increased from 50,225 million pounds in 2008 to 55,470 million in 2022 (Statista, 2013).

These governmental barriers are not exclusive to developed countries with financial leverage; less developed countries are also culprits. For example, despite the weight of the evidence showing the cost controversial input subsidies costs generally outweigh their benefits in Africa (Jayne & Rashid, 2013), governments' economic goals and efforts to win votes, though mostly disguised under the pretext of agricultural modernization, as in the Case of Ghana and Malawi (Denning et al., 2009; Kansanga et al., 2018), have led to the doubling down on such programs in recent years. An assessment of the ten countries that had active input subsidies in Africa Jayne & Rashid (2013) found that their governments spent US$1 billion annually on such programs, amounting to 28.6% of their public expenditures on agriculture (see also Kato & Greeley, 2016; Renick, 2020; Takeshima & Liverpool-Tasie, 2015). The conclusions of these studies have been nothing short of expected: these subsidies barely make the desired impacts beyond appeasing the populist for political gains. Even more worrying is how they impose and entrench dominant ideals, such as high-input farming, that entrap smallholders into conventional food regimes.

The entanglements described thus far raise questions and concerns about the government's role in resistance to sustainable food system transformations. Governments' complicity with corporate elite actors in resistance and status quo entrenchments (Godek, 2021) stains their credibility and commitment to driving positive change. It raises questions on whether they are up to the task or should be trusted to provide the leadership required for food system transformations.

4.1.1.6 Dysfunctional Policy-Science Interface and the Role of Media

Challenges at the interfaces of negotiating and mediating science and policy in food systems are another area of resistance. Food systems science-policy interfaces are dysfunctional, weak, and nonexistent in many areas (Hainzelin et al., 2023; Sibanda & Mwamakamba, 2021; Singh et al.,

2021). A report commissioned by the European Commission (European Commission. Directorate General for Research and Innovation, 2021) to advise on the need, potential, feasibility, options, and appropriate approaches for science-policy interface(s) (SPIs) to support food systems transformation concluded that current interfaces are dysfunctional and ill-suited for radical transformation. Existing platforms, such as the HLPE, were noted to have a limited scope of work and lacked the power and resources to deliver effectively. Other issues identified included gaps in addressing evolving food systems topics, challenges linking or integrating multiple food system concerns/issues, engagement with relevant stakeholders (public, private, civil), and little consistency across SPIs about promoting full transparency (see also Singh et al., 2021). Likewise, Sibanda et al. (2021), in their preparatory work for the UNFSS, noted that despite the role of evidence-based policy dialogue in navigating complex food systems and delivering healthy diets and livelihoods, food policymakers are barely informed of relevant research outputs for informed decision making. These claims all speak to instances of dysfunctional science-policy interfaces, which can create a loophole for powerful actors to undermine transformation by politicizing research in ways that limit translation into policy.

Also significant in this dysfunctionality is the responsibility of the media. The media is a powerful tool in facilitating bringing science and policy into conversation with each other (Boykoff, 2008b, 2008a). However, evidence in the food sector points to a rather halfhearted media serving as a conduit through which science-policy interfaces crack with confusion and doubts around scientific evidence. For example, Almiron and Zoppeddu (2015) reviewed English media in Italy and Spain's coverage of the effects of meat on climate change and found that, contrary to available scientific evidence, there is a weak correlation between climate change and food production in the print media (Willett et al., 2019: see also Kiesel, 2010). Many other studies have alluded to media blind spots, including meat's impact on the environment and health, despite the mounting evidence (Pohjolainen et al., 2016; Sievert et al., 2021). Such limited coverage and doubts breed low consciousness and awareness on the subject, reducing the potential for public pressure for policies that create positive change.

In lieu of these issues, many scientific pieces of evidence fail to make it into the policy space. This situation undermines efforts to drive positive change in the food systems. Thus, experts have concluded that the current landscape of SPIs must be enhanced to deliver the required food system transformations (see Singh et al., 2021). We will return to this in later sections.

4.1.2 Resistance Related to Cultural Dynamics, Norms, and Behavior

In this section, we discuss some of the resistance related to cultural dynamics, norms, and behavior described in the literature.

4.1.2.1 Users/Consumer Values and Lifestyle and Habitus, Norms, Societal Expectations

Within discussions of food systems inertia is the growing acknowledgment of how norms and social expectations and their resultant individual/consumer behaviors and lifestyles influence and resist change (in food systems). In particular, entrenched lifestyle routines described by social and psychological theorists as products of cultural understandings and expectations (Shove et al., 2012) have been identified as sources of inertia for unsustainable food production and consumption trajectories (Sargant, 2014; Shove et al., 2012; Spaargaren et al., 2011). For example, social, personal, and cultural values around eating meat, as shown in the case of Germany (Hübel & Schaltegger, 2022) and Scotland (Macdiarmid et al., 2016) and much of the Western world, continue to reproduce and support the entrenchment of red meat industries. Similar concerns have been found in African cultures, where, for example, meat consumption and fatness (girth) are attached to the social status of wealth, power, and respect (Asamane et al., 2021; Gbejewoh et al., 2022; Tschirley et al., 2014). Consequently, public consumption of red meat is over 300–600% of the EAT-Lancet reference diet in many regions despite the scientific alarms of negative consequences on global climate change and human health (Willett et al., 2019). Amid cultural attachments, not even the birth and promotion of alternative proteins have succeeded in slowing red meat consumption or shown any signs of that effect (Gravely & Fraser, 2018); meat consumption is projected to grow at least 14% by 2030 (compared to the 2018–2020 level) (OECD & FAO, 2021).

Furthermore, studies in sensory and cultural acceptance (Jensen & Lieberoth, 2019; Wilks et al., 2019) show that cultural norms do not just entrench old habits but contribute to resistance. For example, cultural inappropriateness and (un)familiarity with insects in Western societies hinder consumption and eventual transitions to alternative proteins, such as eating insects. Likewise, on the contrary, new and emerging behaviors, like eating ultra-processed foods in developing economies (Baker & Friel, 2016; Moodie et al., 2021), where there are growing incomes and associated cultural changes, have transitioned consumptions toward unsustainable trajectories (Azuike et al., 2011; Baker & Friel, 2016; Dixon, 2009).

These experiences around red meat and alternative proteins, one of the most contested issues in the transition toward healthy diets (Béné & Lundy, 2023), present an essential lesson of social-norm-induced resistance (Almiron & Zoppeddu, 2015; Lea & Worsley, 2001; Rust et al., 2020). Changing consumer behavior is hard enough because culture and associated norms that influence them are deeply entrenched in people's practices. The inertia can be explained by most people preferring to follow the norm (Berger, 2019; DuPuis & Goodman, 2005), reproducing them even when we deem them undesirable (Nyborg et al., 2016). But even more challenging to this effect is the ability of big corporations to identify such sentimental attachments and leverage them to perpetuate their interests through media advertisements or direct engagements with communities through product marketing (Baker et al., 2021; Moodie et al., 2021).

4.1.3 Resistance Related to Capacity and Financial Resources (of the Public Sector)

This section explores some of the documented resistance related to the capacity and financial resources of the public sector.

4.1.3.1 Lack of Human and/or Capital Resources in Government Institutions

Also important to resistance to food system transformation is the lack of the necessary human and capital resources. This resistance is more about how resource inadequacies undermine the creation and execution of actions for transformations and less about direct resistance to change. Yee and Liu (2021) also observed that organizational constraints within government entities in China impede effective governance reforms for food safety enforcement. Other scholars noted concerns about a lack of human and financial capacities, including Pereira and Drimie (2016) in South Africa, where capital and human resource issues have hampered the implementation of food system governance reforms.

Many capacity limitations identified and discussed in the literature, understandably, are financial constraints. For instance, in the assessment of the nutrition transition in Nigeria, Fanzo et al. (2020) found that, despite clear commitments in policy for nutrition changes, the implementation of nutrition policies is hampered by weak implementation capacities through low financial resource allocations at federal and state levels. The underlining discussions of challenges to financing food systems transformation (Díaz-Bonilla, 2023; Limketka et al., 2020), including during UNFSS discussions (Diaz-Bonilla et al., 2023), are a testament to this issue. The declining public purses for agriculture and food are largely blamed for this challenge (HLPE, 2020, 2021). However, the lack of explicit attention to such financial challenges at the subnational levels where true implementation occurs is concerning.

While the lack of financial resources is well acknowledged as a concern for food systems transformations (Millan et al., 2019), one may argue poor and ineffective prioritization of actions is where the challenge lies. The financial backing channeled into harmful incentives (Politico, 2022; see also 4.1.1.5) confirms that resources are available, but governments are ineffective in targeting the right actions to use them wisely. Likewise, as evident in many developing countries, where the lack of human and financial resources is more apparent, uncontrolled corruption within government institutions breeds weak leadership (Amadi & Ekekwe, 2014; Lawal, 2007) that can undermine resource mobilization and implementation processes.

Essentially, this discussion shows that inadequacies in human and financial capacities hinder the transformation of food systems. In particular, such challenges resist transformation as they hamper the design, formulation, implementation, and enforcement of transformational actions.

4.1.3.2 Lack of Know-how (in Government Institutions)

Part of the capacity challenges to food system transformation is the weak knowledge and conceptual understanding of what, when, and how to deliver the transformation (Yee & Liu, 2021; Zerbian et al., 2022). For example, Gillespie et al. (2019) noted that the lack of understanding and knowledge of nutrition (as a multisectoral issue) is a crucial barrier to prioritizing nutrition in India, Nepal, Bangladesh, and Pakistan. When Sonnino et al. (2019) also examined the challenge of changing food systems in over 33 cities across the world, limited understanding and knowledge about food flows and modularity, which indeed are prerequisites to knowing what to change, were noted as critical barriers to any reasonable shift. Knowledge limitations across cities and public entities are also identified and discussed in the cases of Spain and the UK (Zerbian & de Luis Romero, 2021; Zerbian et al., 2022). So, despite the growing commitments to food system transformations at various levels, the knowledge of how to undertake this remains limited within public institutions, which, in many contexts, serve as the flagbearers of change actions.

While the lack of know-how is a widely established barrier (Den Boer et al., 2021; Wu et al., 2015), the underlying causes are debatable. It is simplistic to assume that institutions lack the know-how because the right knowledge is unavailable. To some extent, such an assumption holds some truth as there is undoubtedly no one pathway to (sustainability) transformation (Constance et al., 2018; Garnett, 2013). Yet, in theory, some knowledge exists to guide food systems transformation or at least to set actors on the path to laying foundations for it. This knowledge was evidenced in the many proposals laid out as part of the UNFSS and processes that followed (Fanzo & Davis, 2021; Okoro et al., 2022; Sibanda & Mwamakamba, 2021). Dysfunctionality in mechanisms that make such knowledge accessible to the public sector, such as science policy interface platforms at the subnational levels (Den Boer et al., 2021; Hainzelin et al., 2023; von Braun & Kalkuhl, 2015), contribute to the lack of access to the available knowledge.

The links between the lack of know-how and the resistance to change rest on the power of knowledge. As noted earlier, knowledge and power are intrinsically linked (Anderson et al., 2019), so the lack of know-how is a recipe for constrained power by (public) institutions to deliver sustainable change. Without the right knowledge and conceptual understanding of how food systems work, especially regarding sustainability goals, not even the most well-intentioned political commitments would move the needle of transformation.

4.1.4 Resistance Related to Technological Innovations

This section discusses documented technological politics that currently resist changes in the food system.

4.1.4.1 Technological Path Dependency and Lock-in

Drawing mainly from dominant traditions in the socio-technical transitions, it is argued that once established technologies become embedded in the system, they block alternative development pathways (Friedman & Ormiston, 2022; Geels, 2014). Thus, technological path-dependencies and lock-ins, described as how past innovations and technological commitments have an important bearing on current choices and lock-ins when such past events offer advantages to certain technologies over competitors, are among the most discussed resistances to change (Conti et al., 2021; Friedman & Ormiston, 2022; Goldstein et al., 2023; Oliver et al., 2018). In food system, for example, IPES-Food (2016) have described how individual farms and entire regions such as the US "corn belt" or the Argentine "soy belt" – have become dependent on highly specialized production of specific commodity crops, rooted through accumulated investments in specialized commodity-specific skills, training, equipment, networks, and retail relationships. In this case, the highly specialized supply chains and infrastructure, with production practices fitting to each other, allow industry actors to work very efficiently – even if within an unsustainable system. Similar technological lock-ins have been noted by Pignatti et al. (2015) on how conventional irrigation systems limit innovations, as well as by Aramyan et al. (2021) and Kirchherr et al. (2018) on how circular economy approaches are continually relegated to niches due to incompatibility with existing infrastructures. With these sorts of structures, any thoughts of change are considered distractive from the norm and actively resisted.

Technological path-dependencies and lock-ins of food systems are beyond decisions of single innovations; they are evident in broader innovation systems. For example, drawing on Systems of Innovation (SI), Vanloqueren and Baret (2009) show that agricultural innovation systems have suppressed agroecological innovations at the expense of genetic engineering. Predicated on the paradigm of growth and productivity, genetic engineering benefited from the creation of a broad, favorable environment, which included funds, specific infrastructures (such as the European Molecular Biology Laboratory), a workforce trained in molecular techniques, and strong policy support across countries, and internationally through the UN systems and CGIAR. The results have been national and international innovation systems path dependent on genetic engineering, including patenting of innovations, contrary to the democratic, community-centered ideals of alternatives such as agroecology (Altieri, 1995; Miles et al., 2017a). These experiences have resisted agroecology innovations, leaving them to the margins as deeply rooted dominant structures of genetic engineering blossoms(see also Klerkx & Begemann, 2020; Leeuwis et al., 2021; Vanloqueren & Baret, 2009).

Political economy scholars, in line with their long history of examining society's historical and structural dynamics (Anderson & Leach, 2019; De Schutter, 2017), have discussed how these lock-ins and dominance emanate. The scholarship has argued that today's food systems, like most aspects of society, are dominated by neoliberal capitalist ideals, which by virtue favor the most economically fittest technologies at the expense of other potentially sustainable alternatives (ETC Group, 2022; Hutter & Lawrence, 2021; Vanloqueren & Baret, 2009). The uncritical processes have positioned technological innovations such as mechanization and bio-technologies and now emerging digitalization as the transformative force for food systems without considering their broader social impacts (Abdulai, 2022; Barrett et al., 2022; Herrero et al., 2020). Hence, in spite of the beaming agri-food innovation pipeline (Herrero et al., 2020; IPES-Food, 2023), the economic and profit ideals that underpin the system unsurprisingly make only those with the most financial sense or those that make only incremental improvements without substantial shifts emerge successfully (Béné, 2022). The effect of this kind of favoritism is lock-ins and path dependencies that have created innovation processes and outcomes that resist and entrench unsustainable trajectories (ETC Group, 2022; Schneider et al., 2020) and prevent sustainable alternatives.

4.1.4.2 Absence of Alternative Technological Solutions

Another important area of technological politics that drives resistance to food systems change is the absence of alternatives. The key argument on technological absence is that the conventional dominant regime uses the power to suppress the creation and dissemination of alternative technologies, thereby binding actors to old and unsustainable options rigidities (Goldstein et al., 2023; Hübel & Schaltegger, 2022; IPES-Food, 2016). For example, in Ghana, smallholder farmers adopting conventional green transformation innovations, such as hybrid seeds and chemicals, have been shown to be influenced by a lack of alternatives. In this case, desperate farmers in search of solutions to their many challenges are institutionally locked into unsustainable technologies because of a lack of viable alternatives (Vercillo et al., 2015). Likewise, as Hübel and Schaltegger (2022) found in Germany's meat processing, actors are compelled to use unsustainable supply chains due to a lack of alternatives. The cases are indicative of how absence can perpetuate existing regimes.

While claims of the absence are not untrue, some may note that actual resistance lies in the lack of access to alternatives rather than their absence (Holt-Giménez, 2019; Holt-Giménez & Altieri, 2013). For example, alternative food systems scholars often, understandably, argue that available innovations, such as agroecology, offer holistic alternatives to conventional innovations and are capable of transformative processes, solutions, and outcomes. It is mostly the malignment of those alternatives in current systems where resistance is situated (Altieri, 1995; Holt-Giménez & Altieri, 2013; Khadse et al., 2018). Consequently, the claims of absence are only diversions to justify further development of high-tech solutions instead of promoting proven alternatives that can lead to better outcomes.

That notwithstanding, in whatever form absence is viewed – either as true nonavailability or as political suppression – the lack of alternative technological solutions still poses resistance to transformation. Both dimensions of absence cushion unsustainable food regimes by trapping actors to established and unsustainable innovations.

In this section, we reviewed and discussed some political resistance in food systems across the four domains proposed in the Framework. These discussions show the complexities of political resistance across different domains of food systems. It is evident from the discussions that active resistance and mechanisms of status quo stability hinder sustainable change. The inherent nature of this resistance necessitates efforts to unblock them, which the Framework proposes must start with the creation and maintaining new momentum.

4.2 Issues in Creating and Maintaining New Momentum

As stated earlier, the second stage and process for transforming food systems is creating and maintaining new momentum. We described this process in Section 3.2.2 and further expanded on it in this section. Specifically, we delve deeper into the political actions that (could) create and sustain alternative momentum in the food system (see Table 4 and the discussions that follow).

4.2.1 Creating/Maintaining Momentum through Framing, the Political Economy of Actors, Knowledge, and Evidence

Following the discussion of the political economy of actors' related resistance to food systems change in 4.1, this section discusses the actions of the political economy of actors and the evidence proposed and/or used to create and maintain alternative forces of change in food systems. The actions discussed in this section are largely tailored toward countering the practices and politics of the big corporations introduced in Section 4.1.1 and sowing the seeds for sustainable alternatives.

4.2.1.1 Framing of the Problem and Narratives of Change (Policymakers)

(Re)Framing food system problems and setting out narratives that give currency to the visions of sustainability (Béné et al., 2019; Béné & Lundy, 2023; Fraser et al., 2016; Garnett, 2013) are instrumental steps in sowing the seeds of transformation. We discussed in Section 4.1.1 how big corporations that favor regime structures have shaped and dominated frames of food system crises. Such entrenched narratives, such as the feeding nine billion earlier discussed, can only be countered in practice by new frames and narratives in policy circles that center visions of sustainability (Calo et al., 2021; Holt Giménez & Shattuck, 2011; Holt-Giménez & Altieri, 2013).

To effectively frame alternative food systems narratives of change in policy spaces, the involvement of trusted actors, especially the research community, would be critical. Research within academic institutions, public bodies, civil society organizations, or independent entities can further shape framings of the challenges of dominant regimes while offering narratives from which alternative missions and futures emerge and thrive (see IPES-Food, 2023; Klerkx &

Table 4 Issues in creating and maintaining new momentum

The process	Domains	2. Creating and sustaining new momentum	
		Issues	Selected references
Discursive practices / instrumental power	Framing, the political economy of actors, knowledge, and evidence	• Framing of the problem and narratives of change (policymakers) • Enabling and incentivizing positive contributions from the private sector • Generation of demand for evidence of effectiveness • Incentivizing of horizontal coherence (multi-sectoral coordination) • Advocacy to change priority (civil society)	(Anderson, 2019; Baker, Lacy-Nichols, et al., 2021; Clark et al., 2021; Duncan et al., 2022; Fanzo & Davis, 2021; Gillespie et al., 2013; Giner & Brooks, 2019; HLPE, 2020; IPES-Food & ETC Group, 2021; Swinburn, 2019)
	Cultural dynamics, norms, and behavior	• Creating and raising consumer awareness • Building counter-narratives (civil society, users/consumers)	(Brouwer et al., 2021; Gabe et al., 2021; Lizie, 2012; Nyborg et al., 2016; Sargant, 2014; Spaargaren et al., 2011)

Table 4 (cont.)

The process	Domains	2. Creating and sustaining new momentum	
		Issues	Selected references
Institutional capacity and technology	Capacity and financial resources (of the public sector)	• Leadership and championing • Systemic and strategic capacity building	(Gillespie et al., 2013; Haddad et al., 2016; Kang et al., 2022; Qiao et al, 2019; Schiller et al., 2020; Thow et al., 2022; Zerbian et al., 2022)
	Technological innovation	• Supporting the creation and diffusion of new sustainable innovations • Creating (technological) infrastructure supporting innovations/changes	(Barrett et al., 2022; den Boer et al., 2021a; Herrero et al., 2020; Hubeau et al., 2017; Miles et al., 2017a; Smith, 2006; Stephens, 2021)

Begemann, 2020; Willett et al., 2019). For example, Sen's (1983) valuable research on poverty and famine elaborated on the issues of entitlements and reframed food security discourse from coloristic production to individual entitlements and set the foundation for multidimensional policies and responses to poverty and food security (Carolan, 2013). So, the right positioning of scientific research can propel alternative narratives and visions of food systems to systematic recognition. Nevertheless, the success of problem framing is less about the research (which is at an all-time high in most areas – Bornmann et al., 2021) and more about how it is synthesized into convincing and trusted narratives backed by facts and evidence that can draw decision-makers. The involvement of diverse actors through science-policy interfaces and other multi-stakeholder platforms would be crucial in the framings and narratives that propel sustainable and inclusive visions of food systems transformations (Singh et al., 2021). Recent efforts, such as the HLPE report (HLPE, 2020), in scientifically exploring and framing food system directions offer some prospects for defining the problems and creating alternative narratives of the sustainability of food systems that hold stronger legitimacy.

It is, however, essential to acknowledge that setting out a single common framing for food systems transformation is a near-impossible task, nor should that be the aim. It is vital for policy to embrace the plurality of pathways that may drive food systems toward broader sustainability goals (Duncan et al., 2022; Leach et al., 2020) without necessarily channeling energy into disputations for a single right approach. However, this should not negate the need for choices on root problems to focus on and what narratives policy actors amplify (Béné et al., 2019). There is room for the coexistence of frames in policy circles to bring multiple framings to establish sustainable directions for food systems, and policymakers have critical roles in the process.

4.2.1.2 Enabling and Incentivizing Positive Contributions from the Private Sector

Another political mechanism to create new and alternative momentum is enabling and incentivizing positive contributions from the private sector. The private sector greatly influences the food systems through the resource-rich activities of big corporations and other ways as they interact with many actors. As Gillespie et al. (2013) note, "private effect in food goes beyond the big corporates to include medium-scale and small-scale processors of staple foods, and private health networks that increasingly are involved in the production, marketing, and consumer choice in the purchase of food and other nutrition-relevant goods and services" (p. 558). However, history and experiences have shown that the private sector cannot be trusted to self-directedly pursue positive change, not least when change outcomes stand in contrast to their unwavering profiteering and self-aggrandizing interests (Yates et al., 2021). Hence, enabling and incentivizing the private sector through diverse mediums would be required to keep them within the visions of sustainable food systems.

There are prospects for forward-looking incentives that incline private actors, such as big food corporations, toward sustainable directions. Specifically, certification schemes and public procurement have proven successful in diverse spaces for incentivizing private actors to act right or at least differently from the status quo. For example, public and private fair trade certifications around the world have created an alternative institutional model that changes food companies' practices, at least in theory (Knößlsdorfer et al., 2021; Macdonald, 2007). The adoption of fair trade schemes by companies such as Starbucks, Ben and Jerry, Divine Chocolate, and Dunkin' Donuts – though not without concerns – shows how certification practices can incentivize and nudge private actors toward sustainability. The Starbucks CAFÉ Practices, for instance, have been shown to bring equity to the coffee supply chain by empowering marginalized workers and producers (Macdonald, 2007). These changes are attributable to the certification schemes that keep companies in check as they seek to gain consumer trust.

Another area of enabling and incentivizing changes to private behavior is leveraging the procurement powers of governments to direct sustainable change, that is, sustainable public procurement. Brazil's National School Feeding Program is a typical example of this measure (Kitaoka, 2018; Sidaner et al., 2013). It requires that 30% of the food for school meals be sourced from local family farms, that organic and agroecological products be prioritized, and that products must avoid child labor or harmful pesticides (Azevedo et al., 2023; Soares et al., 2017). With such measures, private actors participating in the program are "forced" to incorporate these sustainability practices into their activities. As governments set the standards, private companies are nudged to alter their practice accordingly.

Other measures such as positive regulations in food environments, food labeling, taxation incentives, and subsidies for sustainable alternatives are avenues to incentivize positive changes from private actors (Giner & Brooks, 2019; Hawkes, 2010; Ngqangashe & Friel, 2022). Systematic reviews of some of these measures have largely concluded that there are overall positive effects for private behavior changes and individual and health outcomes (Acton et al., 2019; Acton & Hammond, 2020; Hashem et al., 2019). For example, a meta-analysis of food labeling interventions by Shangguan et al. (2019) concluded that they influence industry practices to reduce sodium and artificial trans-fat contents. However, some studies have questioned whether measures such as sin taxes influence behaviors, as other evidence has shown no reduction in obesity and other targeted metrics (Haines, 2017). While the evidence is contradictory, their ability to positively influence corporate and individual behaviors toward sustainable goals is relevant in the discussion of food systems transformation.

Essentially, the suit of measures for incentivizing changes in private behaviors is broad. Whatever the nature of incentivization, however, success could depend on a broader enabling environment. Complementary public investment in key public goods, adequate food systems-related infrastructure, agricultural R&D, evidence-based advocacy, payments for ecosystem services, and government institutional flexibility practices have all been suggested in the literature and/or applied in different contexts to create a supporting environment (Baker, et al., 2021; Kennedy et al., 2021; Post et al., 2021).

4.2.1.3 Generation of Demand for Evidence of Effectiveness

Generating demand for evidence of effectiveness is integral to creating and maintaining new momentum for food systems. Evidence of effectiveness is derived from evidence-based policymaking, described as "the use of the best available scientific evidence on the effectiveness of programs, practices, and policies to guide the decision-making process" (Gies et al., 2020, p. 157). Demand for evidence of effectiveness thus justifies sustainable alternatives by supporting them with evidence. This will ensure that only actions that have the potential to lead to sustainability goals are pursued. By depending on evidence to make decisions on alternatives, there may be minimal risk of undertaking actions that entrench unsustainable trajectories.

To generate demand for evidence of effectiveness, research would first be required to produce the needed evidence. Evaluation research has been shown to provide the scope and methods for generating such evidence (Cooper, 2011; Gies et al., 2020). Evaluation of the effectiveness of interventions is a common stay in food systems research and practice (Berti et al., 2004; Mahumud et al., 2022; Thorpe et al., 2021). Most of these researches evaluate the impacts of interventions at the tail end of specific programs. Yet, generating demand for evidence of effectiveness would require deliberate efforts to prove the potential of alternative actions earlier in their conceptions. Novel approaches for delivering these potential evidence, though they may be challenging, must be explored by researchers. Creating a registry for evidence of alternative interventions' effectiveness (Gies et al., 2020) would be helpful as a one-stop access point that can attract actors to use it in decision-making. Such measures must be complemented with educational and accountability measures that draw decisions to use available evidence.

4.2.1.4 Incentivizing of Horizontal Coherence (Multisectoral Coordination)

See Section 4.4 for a detailed discussion on horizontal coherence.

4.2.1.5 Advocacy to Change Priority (Civil Society)

Advocacy to change priorities (by civil society) is a critical mechanism in creating alternative forces in the food system. Food system actors often use advocacy to bring attention to issues of concern. Food CSOs, for instance, have been the most vocal critics of modern food systems through their advocacy activities (MacRae & Abergel, 2012). Through criticisms of the dominant system, CSOs have advocated for changes to priorities and causes of action, with varying degrees of success in nudging change. For example, charting the potential role of civil society movements in the future of food system transformations IPES-Food and ETC Group (2021) documented many victories at local and national levels. Among others, sustained CSO advocacy campaigns have led to a crackdown on corporate-led junk food in countries like Chile, Mexico, and the UK. Advocacy activities of the National Coordination of Peasant Organizations in Mali, such as lobbying, publications, and conferences, are another successful case of their strategy in creating an alternative momentum of change. The organization successfully lobbied the country's government in 2006 to Agricultural Orientation Law. Against the powers of the conventional corporate regime, the law prioritizes peasants and their practices of agroecology and food sovereignty (McKeon, 2014). Other cases of successful advocacies include GM crop uprooting and opposition to life patenting around the world (see also Rose, 2015, for extensive discussion and examples).

Successful advocacies are largely based on the strategies and mechanisms used: evidence-based advocacy is critical. In Canada, for example, the People's Food Policy (PFP) groundbreaking report in 2011 by CSOs synthesized food problems and expanded the public policy frame of food and agriculture as issues of indigenous food sovereignty, sustainable production systems, poverty reduction, and access to sustainably produced food for all – which shifted concentration from the narrowly focused capitalist productivist agriculture system in the country (Barling et al., 2002; Clark et al., 2021; Levkoe & Sheedy, 2018). Discursive progress by civil society in framing food systems change is also evident in language such as "industrial epidemics" and "commercial determinants of health" that have taken center stage in food discourse, thus countering regime discourses and powers of corporate actors (Jahiel & Babor, 2007; Yates et al., 2021). These examples and many others across food systems owe their success to the creation and dissemination of evidence through reports, workshops, articles, and other mediums of communication as used by CSOs to influence changes in policy priorities.

It must be noted that more efforts are needed to ensure the systematic level of success of CSO advocacy due in part to current failures and challenges. First, CSOs have low capacities (in finances and human resources) compared to dominant corporations that drive food systems priority setting (Clayton et al., 2000). Second, the fragmentation of CSO activities around the diverse interests they represent can sometimes undermine the ability to sustain actions for long enough to see change happen (Klassen et al., 2023; Renting & Wiskerke, 2010). Third, and more importantly, advocacy can be, and most times are, toothless as CSOs lack the power to implement change beyond suggestions (MacRae & Abergel, 2012). Nonetheless, advocacies by civil societies and other entities, such as consumers, would be crucial in directing the future trajectories of food systems. Some scholars (e.g., Swinburn, 2019) have expressed hope for civil society to drive food system changes by describing them as a sleeping giant awakening and flexing its muscles to demand government and food industry policy actions (see also IPES-Food & ETC Group, 2021).

4.2.2 Creating/Maintaining Momentum through Cultural Dynamics, Norms, and Behavior

Building on the cultural dynamics related to resistance to food system change discussed in Section 4.1.2, this section discusses documented political actions and strategies that (could) create new momentum of changes in cultural norms and behaviors. These actions described in this section are geared toward creating alternatives that differ and start to compete, as well as potentially changing consumer lifestyles, values, habitus, norms, and societal expectations that resist changes in the system.

4.2.2.1 Creating and Raising Consumer Awareness

One way to create new and alternative momentum in cultural dynamics, norms, and behaviors is by raising consumer awareness of sustainable behaviors. At present, studies show consumers are less aware or hold misconceptions of many issues that have a bearing on their food behaviors, including, for example, the impact of their diets on climate change, land-water use, and biodiversity loss (Brown et al., 2011; Fan, 2021; Kimenju et al., 2005). Thus, awareness programs to increase knowledge of food (practices) and behaviors and norms are critical in nudging sustainable change (Freeland-Graves & Nitzke, 2002; Parsons and Barling (2021) Rowe, 2002). Among others, public information/

campaigns (e.g., UK's Change4Life campaign), interpretive tools that provide information in accessible ways (e.g., dietary guidelines), and labeling, such as front-of-pack traffic light labels, are documented strategies to raise awareness. In the UK, for example, the Love Food Hate Waste awareness campaign – using social media, newsletters, and food gatherings – is credited for changes in individual behavior toward waste, including buying the right food and amounts and using the foods they buy (Quested et al., 2013). Communication through traditional channels (Television, radio, etc.), social media, interpersonal communication (home, school, peer, etc.), group-based approaches through social support networks, and social mobilization through campaigns, special events, and community engagements have been employed in varied spaces by governments and civil societies, especially within the nutrition field (see Gillespie et al., 2013).

Though these awareness strategies are hardly innovative, there is ample evidence of their varied effectiveness in changing behaviors. For instance, a systematic review and meta-analysis conducted on nutrition social behavior change communication (NSBCC) (Mahumud et al., 2022) found that NSBCC helped in nudging behavior change to improve child arthrometric outcomes in the first 1,000 days. Likewise, in Indonesia, mass-media and community-based behavior change campaigns created on the concept of gossip successfully impacted dietary diversity (vegetable intake) and breastfeeding practices (White et al., 2016). The growing engagement of consumers in alternative food systems, such as increased demand for agroecology practices or organic products in the developed world, is also attributed to impacts of awareness of critical food issues, such as environmental impacts and animal welfare (Bui et al., 2016; Schiller et al., 2020). Novel awareness approaches must, however, be continually searched to nudge food system actors toward sustainability.

4.2.2.2 Building Counter-Narratives (Civil Society, Users/Consumers)

Building counter-narratives (by civil society, users/consumers) is an important way to create new and alternative sustainability forces in the food system. As we have established in previous sections, current food systems are dominated by the corporate-led dangerous and reductionist frames of the challenge of productivity, ignoring the equally fundamental inequities in social control over food distribution (Conway & Toenniessen, 1999; Godfray et al., 2010, p. 9). Transforming the food system would, however, require giving particular attention to alternative and counter-narratives that yield potential social and environmental benefits beyond the economic ideals promoted by the main narratives (Anderson & Rivera-Ferre, 2021; Holt-Giménez & Altieri, 2013).

There is no absence of counter-narratives to the neoliberal-driven productivist ideals (Barrett et al., 2022; Brouwer et al., 2021; Leeuwis et al., 2021; Okoro et al., 2022). The entry of food sovereignty, regenerative agriculture, and rights-based approach, which have been championed by organizations such as Via Cepesina and other civil society entities, within the rhetoric of food systems policies and actions are testaments to existing and emerging counter-narratives to the dominant discourse of last five decades (Anderson & Rivera-Ferre, 2021; Claeys, 2013; Haddad & Oshaug, 1998; Holt-Giménez & Altieri, 2013). These counter-narratives have had various successes. Today, for example, food sovereignty has become a global phenomenon and frame that stands in contrast to and challenges the corporate food system with various degrees of success. Not least, the acknowledgment of that frame in the discourses of global forums and among international organizations such as the FAO is a testament to their success (Drummond, 2013). At the local scale, the successes of the Navdanya initiative in India in challenging corporate narratives of GMOs for food security while establishing the critical roles of organic farming and farmer sovereignty is an important case (Thernsjö, 2018; Virmani & François Lépineux, 2015). These experiences show the prospects of grassroots activities in driving shifts in narratives.

However, civil society and consumers require more efforts to create successful counter-narratives that can genuinely compete and, if possible, replace the dominant discourse in the long run. Some possible ways of achieving this goal are through continuous (evidence-based) advocacy around alternative narratives (see 4.2.1.5) and consumer actions that demand transparency and accountability in the food systems (we will return to these points in Section 4.4).

In summary, actions introducing alternative understandings surrounding new and old food practices would provide impetus to shift away from unsustainable norms and behaviors toward sustainable healthy diets. Policy initiatives must take center stage but should be backed by targeted behavior change communication strategies.

4.2.3 Creating/Maintaining Momentum through Capacity and Financial Resources (of the Public Sector)

This section discusses actions to minimize the effects of capacity-related resistance introduced in Section 4.1.3 and create the foundations for sustainable alternatives where public actors can contribute to sustainable futures. The following actions have been documented as (possibly) creating new and alternative capacities in the public sector.

4.2.3.1 Leadership and Championing

A key process of removing, creating new, and maintaining momentum for food system change is through leadership and championing. When the visions of leadership are aligned with sustainable alternatives, they create avenues for championing processes that (can) create new momentum for change. This will partly involve by convening diverse actors around the set vision(s) to create strong alliances (across and between government, civil society, and the private sector) to take timely and decisive action for change (Clark et al., 2021).

Practical experiences across food systems have been documented on how leadership has contributed to or can be leveraged for food systems' actions. In Chile, for instance, food systems leadership manifested through the individual drive, long-term tenacious political commitment by Senator Guido Girardi to redirect that country policy spaces toward healthy diets through the enactment of warning labels on healthy foods, restrictions on marketing to children, healthy school food policies, and taxes on sugary drink (Swinburn, 2019; see also Corvalán Aguilar et al., 2013). As a former doctor and later senator, Girardi proposed and pushed through the now-groundbreaking Nutritional Labeling and Advertising Law. After more than a decade of resistance and opposition by food companies, Girardi pushed through and finally had the law implemented in 2016 – making it the first national effort to truly regulate the practice of big food corporations in the country (Boza et al., 2017; Shepherd, 2018). The success of the Chilean case is an example of how conscious leadership and championing can sow the seeds for food system change.

Though leadership and championing of food systems change are essential at international, national, and subnational levels (Haddad et al., 2016; Hebinck et al., 2018; von Braun et al., 2023), it is important to develop stronger systems closer to areas where actions take place. Since jurisdictional and implementation powers rest with subnational governments (and in large countries, states/provinces), the opportunity for them to lead on policy and fiscal actions is crucial to transformation (Swinburn et al., 2015). For instance, Clark et al. (2021) described food leadership efforts that led to the emergence of France's first "organic village" in Correns. The creation of the food movement within a governance structure of equitable participation (by gender, age, paysans, business owners, unemployed residents, etc.) was initiated and championed by the mayor (a winemaker himself), who, by prior experience, aimed to counter the negative impacts of modern agriculture on livelihoods (see also Clément, 2019). Sarabia et al. (2021) and Zerbian and de Luis Romero (2021) also showed that leadership at city and local levels in Spain has contributed to alternative food systems visions. These experiences cement the need to strengthen leadership efforts at the base of the food system, which could enhance grassroots-led championing.

Despite the role of championing and leadership in triggering change, it is often an overlooked piece in food systems (Kang et al., 2022), especially at the local level, where the outcomes of transformations become visible. So, efforts that facilitate the creation of leaders and champions within food systems must be encouraged at all levels, including through systemic and strategic capacity building in the public sector.

4.2.3.2 Systemic and Strategic Capacity Building

Another mechanism to create and maintain new momentum for food system change is deliberate systemic and strategic capacity building of public sector entities. The concept of capacity building is highly debated, as it is often used loosely to describe training, especially in the development field (Babu, 2020; Den Boer et al., 2021). Our view of capacity building is derived from Potter and Brough (2004), who described it as enhancing structures, systems and roles, staff and facilities, skills, and tools of organizations and entities. Systematic capacity building is thus the diverse skills, instincts, abilities, processes, and resources needed by (public sector) organizations and entities to enhance the creation and maintenance of alternative food system actions. It involves mechanisms of information flows, money, and managerial decision-making (Gillespie et al., 2013). Strategic capacity is decision-making forums or multi-stakeholder platforms for holding food systems discussions (Gillespie et al., 2013). So, when we think of systematic and strategic capacity building, we refer to efforts that enhance the capabilities, processes, and mechanisms within the public sector as they relate to food systems.

(Food system) Capacity building is inherent in most development interventions in the developing world – where this challenge is more pressing (Babu, 2020; Masters et al., 2018; Morkel & Ramasobama, 2017; Sako, 2006; Suzanne, 2004). However, continuous gaps in capacities may indicate a need to redirect (food system) capacity building away from the current dependence on international development, primarily short-lived, to more sustainable alternatives. Governments taking up critical roles in capacity building could safeguard long-term sustainability (Qiao et al., 2019; Wu et al., 2015) while reducing external dependence on other parties to drive change efforts.

Though less explored, a strategic focus on regional food systems entities and corresponding capacity building at that level could help the public sector offset some of the challenges. Some governance scholars have suggested regional approaches to strengthen capacities toward food systems transformation (Blay-Palmer et al., 2018; Clancy & Ruhf, 2010; Thow et al., 2022). Regionalization of capacity needs and solutions based on key practical food systems features may minimize the resource strain of fragmented processes at the local level. In the Pacific Island region, for example, the Pacific Community's "Food Systems Program" (a regional platform) provided technical support and resources for countries through adaptable templates, training, workshops, monitoring frameworks, and data, which allowed countries to draw on pooled regional expertise to address common challenges and as an appropriate response and support in the context of a lack of capacity (generally) at the national level (Thow et al., 2022). Some public policy scholars are, however, critical of competition and conflicts with subregional and higher-level entities and the lack of jurisdictional powers required to enact change that has characterized regionalized governance efforts (Börzel & Risse, 2019; Stubbs, 2008). Providing regional entities with legislative backing would institutionalize their governance actions, which could further solidify and justify a focus on capacity building at that level.

4.2.4 Creating/Maintaining Momentum through Technological Innovations

This section discusses some of the (proposed) technological actions (politics) for creating and maintaining new momentum for food systems transformation. We describe two key actions from that literature that could begin to sow the seeds for dismantling the resistance discussed in Section 4.1.4 and lay a foundation for sustainable alternative food systems.

4.2.4.1 Supporting the Creation and Diffusion of New Sustainable Innovations

Supporting the creation and diffusion of new sustainable innovations can have differing roles in transforming food systems (Barrett et al., 2022; Herrero et al., 2020; Khan et al., 2021). Food system transformations in the last century, including the Green Revolution (Evenson, 2003), the biotechnology revolution (Herring & Paarlberg, 2016), and the now-believed digital revolution (Barrett & Rose, 2020; Birner et al., 2021), have all taken off on the back of technological innovations. These, however, have not always been a straightforward process as their long-term negative social and environmental consequences (Carolan, 2018a, 2013; Patel, 2013) cast doubt on their ability to deliver sustainable change. The "supposed successes" of these technologies, at least from the metrics of proponents (e.g., increased outputs – Evenson, 2003), together with the associated financial motivations of incumbents (ETC Group, 2022), explain why technological innovations would remain a part of every push for food system change (Herrero et al., 2020). In a review of innovations that may transition food systems, Herrero et al. (2020) identified 75 broad technologies spanning the entire food chain at different stages of development. However, it is an open secret that only the fittest innovations in terms of profitability are pursued creation, while sustainable alternatives are relegated to the background (Canfield et al., 2021a; ETC Group, 2022; McMichael, 2021; Montenegro de Wit & Iles, 2021). So, a move to sustainable innovations would require drastic changes to how we finance this important element of food systems.

A key way to change this trend and create new momentum is creative financial schemes and a re-orientation of motives and success metrics for innovations to encourage sustainable alternatives (Herrero et al., 2020; Mazzucato, 2016). Among others, alternative social finance, through community investments, ethical banking, alternative currencies, microfinance, social impact bonds, venture philanthropy, and impact investing, is beginning to gain traction alternatives to improve sustainability outcomes of food systems innovations (Feng et al., 2022; Stephens, 2021). By the patience embedded in these schemes, alternatives can get enough time to build on metrics different from conventional profits (Stephens, 2021). Other financial strategies are encouraged, such as governments tailoring subsidies, procurement processes, and tax incentives to favor emerging sustainable innovations (Khan et al., 2021). Public investment in technology development, when tied to social license and technology acceptability within responsible innovation principles and public dialogue, has also been suggested to push innovations toward sustainable directions (Herrero et al., 2020; Kemper & Ballantine, 2017; Miles et al., 2017a; Stilgoe et al., 2013; Troise et al., 2021). However, these initiatives remain propositions or niches at best, in most cases with limited impacts, as corporate-driven innovation systems continue to dominate and resist change.

At the broader scale, a shift toward a "wide-tech" paradigm – highly decentralized innovation practices based around macro-technological changes for microenvironments (i.e., local farms, abattoirs, or fisheries) – is proposed as a way forward to sustainable innovations in food systems (ETC, 2009). This aligns with the alternative food systems, where diversified and decentralized innovation in spaces areas such as organic farming and agroecology has created some successful momentum for change (Khadse et al., 2018; Val, 2023). For example, experimental evidence from eight African countries showed decentralized innovation systems promote the diffusion of crop management innovations – but successes were moderated by specific dimensions of ex-ante social capital (Pamuk & Rijn, 2018). These technological innovations, if well implemented within alternative frameworks of financing and stakeholder engagements, could have kick-starting effects for transformative innovations.

Essentially, supporting the creation of alternative sustainable innovations would require devising alternative financial schemes that incorporate values such as environmental sustainability and social impacts into the assessment of success. Opening the current centralized innovation system-controlled profit-hungry corporations into a decentralized network of diverse innovations could also redirect the innovations pathways. However, the success of such a shift must also be backed by infrastructure supporting emerging sustainable innovations/changes.

4.2.4.2 Creating (Technological) Infrastructure Supporting Innovations/Changes

Part of forming the foundation for food systems entails creating supporting infrastructures for sustainable alternative technologies and innovations (Marsden et al., 2018; Popkin & Reardon, 2018; Ruben et al., 2021). Evidence shows that the diffusion of digital innovations has been slower than expected among smallholder farmers in Africa due in part to weak supporting internet and telecommunication infrastructures (Tsan et al., 2019). These struggles offer a great example of why supporting infrastructures is a prerequisite for any attempt to shift the innovations in the food systems. Hence, Marsden et al. (2018) have argued that governments, who have mostly been at the forefront of food-relevant infrastructures due to market disinterest in the area, need to create and encourage new forms of both physical and social infrastructures, which they term as the "missing middle." (Marsden et al., 2018).

Infrastructure responsibilities, however, cannot be left to governments alone; the private sector can reasonably support providing some supporting infrastructures needed for food systems change, such as telecommunication (Pingali, 2007; Post et al., 2021). The role of the private actor is due to their financial and market powers, and governments have limited resources (Gillespie et al., 2013). Government regulation of their activities would, however, be required to avoid exploitation of critical services at the expense of broader social good that food systems transformation must aim to achieve.

In this subsection, we have discussed the multiple dimensions of creating and maintaining new momentum for food systems. We have shown how this important step is achievable through various political actions, including alternative narratives that center on sustainability, leadership and championing efforts by governments and individuals, novel, decentralized processes of technological innovations, and positive incentivization of private sectors.

However, alternatives created through these efforts are only as good as they are convincing enough as sustainable options to draw interest within the regime.

4.3 Issues in Converting New Momentum into Sustainable Options

This section discusses the specific political actions (used) to convert new momentum into sustainable options. Having introduced the different actions for creating and maintaining new momentum in the preceding section, this section discusses actions across the four domains that could convert the seeds of transformation sown in stage two (Section 4.2) into broader systematic level options. Table 5 highlights these specific political actions, which we expand on in the rest of the section.

4.3.1 Converting New Momentum through Framing, the Political Economy of Actors, Knowledge, and Evidence

This section discusses some of the political economy of actors, knowledge, and evidence mechanisms to convert new momentum into sustainable options. Building largely on the discussions of the politics of corporations, governments, and other actors in Sections 4.1.1 and 4.2.1, specific ways to ensure alternative frameworks, knowledge, and practices translate into system-level options are presented in this section.

4.3.1.1 Translation of New Framing and Agenda into Concrete Policies

Translation of new framing and agenda into concrete policies is required to ensure alternative narratives and ideas become available options in the food system – to potentially replace unsustainable dominant policies that favor the corporate actors. Without policy backing, most sustainability promises would remain abstract statements of good intentions without clear, practical steps to implementation and action (Oliver et al., 2018). Policy scholars (e.g., Bifulco, 2016; Milat & Li, 2017) have thus emphasized translating framings and agendas into policy as instrumental in driving public and private actions, including in areas of food (Ajates Gonzalez et al., 2018; Kanter et al., 2016), in countering entrenched policies of conventional regimes. This involves using policy instruments (Tummers, 2019) to institutionalize sustainable alternatives. Among others, national food policies, legislations, regulations, and sector-specific policymaking processes are potential avenues to translate framing into concrete and actionable policies.

Table 5 Issues in converting new momentum into sustainable options

Domains	The process	3. Converting new momentum into sustainable options	
		Issues	Selected references
Discursive practices / instrumental power	Framing, political economy of actors, knowledge, and evidence	• Translation of new framing and agenda into concrete policies • Create political coalitions in support of change • Evidence-based documentation of coverage, scale, and quality (scientific community) • Research for alternative food system configurations and 'preferred solutions	(Alroe et al., 2016; Anderson et al., 2019; Aramyan et al., 2021; Fanzo et al., 2021; Gonzalez et al., 2018; HLPE, 2022; IPES-Food & ETC Group, 2021; Lam et al., 2022; Miles et al., 2017a; Swinnen, 2018)
	Cultural dynamics, norms, and behavior	• Encouraging the role of civil society and individuals in changing societal values (e.g., political consumerism) • Alignment of consumer demand with food systems sustainability objectives	(Aldrovandi et al., 2015; Aramyan et al., 2021; Dubuisson-Quellier et al., 2011; Evans & Miele, 2017; Ferraboschi et al., 2022; Gunderson, 2014; Holzer, 2006; Richardson & Fernqvist, 2022; Vermeir et al., 2020)

Institutional capacity and technology	Capacity and financial resources (of the public sector)	• Delivery and operational capacity around compliance and enforcement • Identifying new forms of resource mobilization	(Gillespie et al., 2013; Mvondo, 2009; Park & Kim, 2020; Yee & Liu, 2021)
	Technological innovation	• Alignment of innovations with food systems sustainability indicators • Creating a business case for innovation using financial instruments	(Ajates, 2022; de Adelhart Toorop et al., 2021; Ferraboschi et al., 2022; Herrero et al., 2020; Limketka et al., 2020; Maltais & Nykvist, 2020; Mazzucato, 2016; Poponi et al., 2022; Silvestri et al., 2024; Stephens, 2021)

Food systems literature offers successful examples of translating alternative agendas into concrete policies. For instance, in Brazil, sustainability ideals were successfully translated into public through the National Policy for Agroecology and Organic Production (PNAPO). This followed concerted advocacy and push by CSOs in the country. Through this policy, the National Plan for Agroecology and Organic Production was established, and funding was allocated to support agroecological research, technical assistance, and infrastructure development. Evidence suggests these measures have led to an increased uptick of transitions to agroecology among smallholders in the country (De Molina et al., 2019; Niederle et al., 2023; Van den Berg et al., 2022), thus challenging the established incumbent big ag actors. Similarly, concerted efforts by CSOs led to the translation of values of local, organic, and sustainability into a National school program. This was culminated by the 2015 law by the government that school meals prioritize organic and local, with at least 40% coming from organic farming (Morgan & Sonnino, 2013; Rossi et al., 2021). Likewise, policy initiatives such as sugar taxes and labels (Grunert et al., 2014) – many of which have been discussed earlier in Section 4.2 – draw on certain sustainability visions to mandate private actors to put certain information that could influence consumer decisions. These cases show the role of laws and their accompanying propositions in translating alternative values into policy. These policies create the environment for alternatives to become options that could counter the dominance of powerful corporations discussed in Section 4.1.1. As with agroecology in Brazil and school food in Italy, embedded sustainability ideas help protect alternative practices and provide room for them to thrive – at least within the practicality of their struggle in the global neoliberal, capitalist food regime.

Care is, however, needed when translating sustainable food systems framings into policies due in part to the risk of co-optations and dilution of principles. For example, studies have revealed that efforts to shift away from conventional food systems in the United States through organic farming and school food programs have failed in part due to co-optation and dilution with neoliberal values, such as profit-making and capital accumulation (Allen & Guthman, 2006; Guthman, 2008). Similarly, Crosskey (2016) noted the French government's use of agroecology as a catchphrase to disguise continuous support for large monoculture and highly industrialized models. These experiences necessitate checks when translating alternative agendas into policies. When provided the proper legislative backing, independent science-policy interface platforms can provide such necessary checks (Hainzelin et al., 2023; Singh et al., 2021; Turnhout et al., 2021).

In essence, policy processes cautiously created on sustainable visions across scales are needed to translate alternative momentum into options. Political coalitions for change could further provide the needed push for policies that align with sustainable food systems.

4.3.1.2 Create Political Coalitions in Support of Change

Creating political coalitions in support of change is a crucial political process that can translate alternative sustainability ideals into options. Coalitions in this context refer to partnerships among distinct food systems actors to coordinate action in pursuit of shared alternative visions (cf Fox, 2010). The role of political coalitions cannot be overstated in light of the power, influence, and activities of big corporations that resist food systems change. The dominance and entrenchment of corporate actors and their values in food systems mean that no single entity stands a chance to compete or make meaningful change. However, as Rose (2000, pp. 213–214), quoted in Hassanein (2003, p. 82), argued, movements turn to stand a bigger chance when they become coalitions. Coalition building, which brings multiple interests, organizations, and values, and the convergence of actions, strategies, and resources (Hassanein, 2003), offers some pathways for collective efforts. It allows for a stronger voice and resources to advocate and drive desirable change. A coalition with the right partners, for example, would create access to financial as well as operational resources and may eventually link to the broader enabling environment (Aramyan et al., 2021; Swinburn, 2019) for alternatives to thrive and compete against dominant actors and practices.

Successful examples of food system coalition wins are documented in the alternative food movements. The case of Via Campesina, as discussed earlier, is a typical example of global coalition success for food system change. Likewise, the Community Food Security Coalition (CFSC) in the United States is another excellent example. The CFSC's diverse membership includes more than 500 organizations that address anti-hunger, community development, sustainable agriculture, and urban agriculture/community gardening issues. By bringing multiple organizations under the umbrella of promoting community food security in its broadest definition, the coalition has had a prominent voice on issues relevant to their area while also pulling a larger resource pool to support programs. The results have been, among others, successful lobbying for the 2010 Healthy, Hunger-Free Kids Act, which prompted legislative change by funding farm-to-school programs and the Fruit and Vegetable Program to make products more accessible to schoolchildren (Berman, 2011; Gottlieb & Fisher, 1996; Winne, 2005). Many other coalitions around specific food systems issues and contexts are evident at international, national, and subnational levels, with varying degrees of change impacts, such as the Coalition for Healthy School Food in Canada (see Field & Webb, 2022; Hernandez et al., 2018) and the CSA Network in UK society (see Bonfert, 2022).

These assumed successes of these coalitions and many others have certainly caught the attention of food systems transformation actors, leading to political interest in the mechanism. The formation of the "Coalition for Food Systems Transformation Through Agroecology" from the UNFSS process, among 28 others around specific issues and lines of action,[3] is crucial for change. If well managed, these coalitions could provide the impetus to drive sustainable change across diverse issues to deliver holistic and systemic food systems transformation. Systemic-based alliances that bring people of diverse food system interests and values together are, however, required for more radical and deep-rooted change.

While political coalitions are expected to drive food systems transformation, their formation, creation, and operations are usually characterized with challenges. First, there is no single vision of sustainable food systems (Béné et al., 2019), which creates a wide diversity of actors with interests that may become difficult to reconcile. Second, the diversity of entities within coalitions could potentially create undesirable politics that deviate attention from the core values of change (see Fox, 2010; Gawerc, 2020; Rose, 2000). The success of coalitions could still be maximized by sharing good practices (Blay-Palmer et al., 2016) and following successful practices of others (Prost, 2019).

4.3.1.3 Evidence-based Documentation of Coverage, Scale, and Quality (Scientific Community)

Evidence-based documentation of coverage, scale, and quality of alternative policies and practices can enhance the conversion of new sustainability momentum into available options. Aligning alternative food innovations, practices, capacities, and framings as sustainable options requires continuous research and evidence (Fanzo et al., 2021; McDermid et al., 2023; Schwarz et al., 2021). In their work on the politics of undernutrition reduction, Gillespie et al. (2013) discussed knowledge and evidence in converting new momentum into results. They note that implementation research (what works, why, and how), monitoring of program coverage, and evaluations of programs to learn and improve them are critical to showing viability and scalability. Such evidence would be critical to justifying alternatives and how they better the practices promoted by corporations and other unsustainable actors.

---

[3] www.unfoodsystemshub.org/hub-solution/coalitions-of-action/en.

Evidence-based documentation of alternative is already practiced in the food space. There is growing attention to feasibility studies and formative research, process evaluations, costing studies, monitoring research, and evaluation studies within the food systems (see Gillespie et al., 2013). Within these spaces, governments, researchers, and civil society organizations play crucial roles in evidence documentation in support of interventions (Bhutta et al., 2013; Fanzo et al., 2021; HLPE, 2022). The research of scholarly communities in alternative food system networks offers a basis for how evidence documentation is and should be done. The expansion of interest and practices in these ideals, in parallel to the conventional regimes, could be attributed to scholarships that document their merits, which CSOs leverage for advocacy (Altieri, 1995; Bonfert, 2022; Holt-Giménez & Altieri, 2013; Raja et al., 2017).

More targeted and intentional documentation of evidence related to sustainability dimensions of alternative actions is, however, needed for a sustainable food system transformation (HLPE, 2022; Singh et al., 2021). There are lessons to learn from the alternative food research community and civil society actors. These actors have had experiences with evidence-based documentation of coverage, scale, and quality of specific initiatives such as CSA, agroecology, organic agriculture, and school food programs (see for review Enthoven & Van den Broeck, 2021; Kerr et al., 2021; Martinez, 2010) partly as mechanism to justify relevance, attract more funding and followers (Pitt & Jones, 2016). However, the struggle of these alternative food systems in is displacing or even effectively competing with the dominant regime actors and practices mean their approaches to evidence documentation may benefit novel methods going forward.

More consolidated research efforts are needed to justify alternatives as sustainable options that genuinely differ from the corporate status quo. This is where the research community can play a critical role by providing independent evidence. The monitoring framework proposed by Fanzo et al. (2021) for evidence-based policymaking in the lead-up to Agenda 2030 is an example of how consolidated documentation of evidence could be shaped. With a set of research-informed indicators, the framework provides a critical lens for assessing actions undertaken to attain healthy diets in a sustainable, resilient, just, and equitable manner (Fanzo et al., 2021). The proposed indicator systems may be worth following but must be enhanced by targeting them toward agreed sustainability processes and outcomes. Bringing such a monitoring system into practice would likely be hampered by ineffective data collection and analysis in food systems, including cost and lack of uniformity of collection. Hence, a key part of this documentation is to build mechanisms to enhance quality data collection and analysis for food systems (Fan, 2021; Fanzo et al., 2021; HLPE, 2022).

There is no shortage of research on food systems, but their potential to highlight the value of sustainable alternatives is far from ideal. Moving forward, normative sustainability goals must guide evidence-building, data collection, curation, and consolidation to make them relevant to systemic decision-making. Also important is research that uncovers alternative food system configurations and solutions.

4.3.1.4 Research for Alternative Food System Configurations and Preferred Solutions

Research for alternative food system configurations and preferred solutions would be integral to converting alternative momentum into sustainable options. While there is extensive print media and research on food insecurity issues, there is far less consideration of what an effective local food system might look like (Roggio & Evans, 2022). Research activities that aim to uncover the best arrangements and combinations of food systems' solutions and clarify what sustainability visions and/or goals actions that meet the visions of sustainability set out in stage two of the Framework are thus necessary to provide alternatives to regime politics.

As we already established, what constitutes sustainable food systems and their attributes extensively vary by scholarship (Béné et al., 2019; Constance et al., 2018; Eakin et al., 2017; Fraser et al., 2016; Garnett, 2013). Hence, it only makes sense to have deliberate research portfolios that clarify what configurations would make for a better following, that is, can easily attract potential followers. In this regard, evidence-based presentation of alternatives would likely increase the chance of acceptance and diffusion into the broader regime, thereby moving sustainable configurations beyond niches to becoming the norm (Aramyan et al., 2021; Maye, 2013).

The food space acknowledges and supports the need to research alternative food system configurations and preferred solutions. The growing interest in trade-offs and prioritizing food systems actions based on sustainability goals (Tälle et al., 2019; Vågsholm et al., 2020) speaks to this point. Trade-offs and synergy analysis, when focused on the values of sustainable food futures, can facilitate the detailed assessment options from which the best configurations and solutions can emerge. We will return to a more detailed discussion of trade-offs in Section 4.4.

4.3.2 Converting Momentum through Cultural Dynamics, Norms, and Behavior

This section discusses proposed cultural dynamics, norms, and behaviors that (could) convert momentum into sustainable food system options. The focus here is political actions that can facilitate the cultural and behavioral visibility of sustainable alternatives in the food system.

4.3.2.1 Encouraging the Role of Civil Society and Individuals in Changing Societal Values (e.g., Political Consumerism)

Following on from the discussion of the CSO's role in championing actions that shape societal behaviors in Section 4.2.2, these organizations and individuals can facilitate converting culture and behavioral momentum into sustainable options. Innovation diffusion theory shows that a critical mass of connected people adopting a new (sustainable) behavior can spread a norm change through a social network (Rogers, 1983; Ying & Mengqing, 2011). Such critical mass, however, would require changing the social values toward the alternative visions that underpin new behaviors (Shove et al., 2012). Meanwhile, changing social values is an audacious task due to the cultural, historical, and spiritual entrenchments. We have already discussed the role of civil society in shaping norms through evidence-based advocacy (*4.2.1.5*), so we will focus on the important connected outcomes of increased consumer engagement that may emanate from such advocacies.

Civil society advocacies bring diverse (alternative sustainable) options to light as relevant, at least in the eyes of consumers, allowing them to move from being passive consumers to becoming active food systems (De Schutter, 2014; Jacobsen & Dulsrud, 2007). Consumers' interest in key issues is a form of political consumerism, which scholars have described as market-oriented engagements emerging from societal concerns associated with production and consumption (Boström & Micheletti, 2019). Consumers use purchasing power and sometimes protest to shape food system actions (Holzer, 2006; Hossain & Scott-Villiers, 2019; O'Brien & Macoun, 2022). Individuals avoiding certain brands based on poor environmental reputations or championing the buying of eco-friendly products are examples of political consumerism (Boström & Micheletti, 2019). Ethical food labeling, such as organic, fair trade, and halal, can also be attributed to active engagement by consumers and their demand for change in the food systems (Evans & Miele, 2017; Keller et al., 2017). Through such actions, consumers can demand accountability from producers and decision-makers and can also shape broader societal values regarding certain food system activities.

While political consumerism is extensively discussed positively as a pathway for exerting control in the food systems and potentially shaping societal values, some have quickly labeled it a mechanism for the "educated consumer" (Zorell, 2019). It requires some level of education and privileges to practice fully. However, not all consumers have the proper knowledge and socio-economic conditions to become genuine political consumers. Likewise, consumers are increasingly perceived as malleable as their actions are shaped by marketing and advertising systems that undermine their knowledge's value and potential for informed decision-making, even for the most educated (Roggio & Evans, 2022). The rise of unsustainable nutrition transitions through the consumption of ultra-processed food in many LMICs (Azuike et al., 2011; Baker & Friel, 2016) speaks to the risks and challenges consumer actions may pose to sustainable food futures. Efforts are therefore needed to align consumer demands to sustainability objectives.

4.3.2.2 Alignment of Consumer Demand with Food Systems Sustainability Objectives

We have already highlighted how political consumerism could be leveraged to change social values. Building political consumerism requires aligning consumer demand with food systems' sustainability objectives. This entails instilling values that amplify consumer actions in line with sustainability goals, as set out in alternative visions of food systems. The rise of terms like "sustainable and ethical consumption" (Friel et al., 2014; Herrero et al., 2023; Sargant, 2014; Van Gameren et al., 2015) and "environmentally sustainable consumption" (Vermeir et al., 2020) is an example of such alignment. Extensive discussions exist on the alignment demands to sustainable consumption, and we do not wish to revisit these (see Reisch et al., 2013; Sargant, 2014; Verain et al., 2015; Vermeir et al., 2020). Within these discussions, however, information-based instruments (e.g., food labels), market-based initiatives (e.g., taxes), direct regulations (e.g., control of the advertising of unhealthy foods and drinks), and "nudges" (e.g., operation buy local campaigns) are commonly used and/or proposed to align consumer demand with sustainability issues such as health, GHG emissions, food waste, and labor rights (Reisch et al., 2013; see also Vermeir et al. 2020 for extensive discussions of mechanisms of promoting pro-environmental sustainable food consumption).

It is important to understand that alignment to sustainability may not happen until the right socioeconomic conditions are in place. Food product prices and incomes influence consumers' choices (Andreyeva et al., 2010; Cornelsen et al., 2015; Green et al., 2013), which could hinder efforts to align consumer demands to sustainability. For example, studies show that some consumers resort to potentially unsustainable consumption behaviors in desperation as food prices increase (Hossain & Scott-Villiers, 2019). Likewise, as discussed in earlier sections, consumer awareness programs would be crucial to bridge the gaps between evidence and public perceptions regarding key sustainability issues. Hence, effectively aligning consumer demands with sustainability objectives would require broader socioeconomic development, which may entail enhancing the capacities of public sector entities to support grassroots consumer initiatives.

4.3.3 Converting Momentum through Capacity and Financial Resources (of the Public Sector)

This section discusses actions in capacity and final resources that (could) convert momentum into sustainable food system options. The focus here is political actions to enhance the capacity and resources for public actors to effectively guide the uptake of sustainable alternatives.

4.3.3.1 Delivery and Operational Capacity around Compliance and Enforcement

Delivery and operational capacity around compliance and enforcement is vital to ensuring food system businesses and other actors stay in line with sustainability requirements (Pudjiastuti, 2021). Scholars have long emphasized the critical roles of capacities of the public sector for implementation and enforcement effectiveness (Mvondo, 2009; Verbruggen, 2013; Wilkinson et al., 2014; Wu et al., 2015). In the food system, regulatory compliance and enforcement capabilities are needed to keep practices regime actors in check and facilitate the activities of alternatives (Den Boer et al., 2021; Gillespie et al., 2013; Singh et al., 2021). In their proposal for processes needed for nutrition transition, Gillespie et al. (2013) outlined three key capacities required for scaling implementation and enforcement of nutrition actions: individual capacity by way of methods and skills, organizational capacity by way of staff and infrastructure, and systemic capacity by way of structure, systems, and roles (see Gillespie et al., 2013). Public-sector entities must develop these capacities to ensure that food systems laws can be enforced and that infringements adequately deal with appropriate compliance and enforcement actions.

Capability building is already evident in many areas, including, for example, (international) development activities within countries that cater to the operational mechanisms of the public organization (Hope Sr, 2009; Wenzel, 2007). Country experiences with food safety regulations, enforcement, and compliance offer valuable examples that could be extended to broader sustainability goals. Today, the majority of countries have established the architecture of national food control systems with dedicated agencies for inspection, monitoring, and enforcement (WHO, 2025). Brazil's National Sanitary Surveillance Agency (ANVISA), for example, uses risk-based inspections, digital tools, surveillance, capacity building of decentralized actors, and policing to facilitate food safety compliance and enforcement (Dimas Augusto & Rafaela Marinho, 2024; Seta et al., 2017). Though not without challenges, the food safety enforcement and compliance mechanism could provide a basis for building delivery and operational capacities for sustainability-oriented initiatives.

Establishing legislation, creating dedicated agencies, and decentralizing compliance and enforcement that support more effective delivery are important. Similarly, sustainability-inclined training programs and building technical expertise of relevant agencies are of utmost relevance in this context. New public programs can help minimize the greenwashing of sustainability that growing voluntary private sector regulations and modes of enforcement have created (Fulponi, 2006; Guo et al., 2019; Henson & Reardon, 2005; Verbruggen, 2013). Enhancing the public resources base could position countries to build the required capabilities.

4.3.3.2 Identifying New Forms of Resource Mobilization

The need for diverse resources in program delivery and implementation (Bhatia & Ghanem, 2019; FAO, 2019), coupled with their lack thereof in the public sector, necessitates identifying new forms of resource mobilization to scale sustainable alternatives. In particular, financial resources to support sustainable alternatives are needed (Apampa et al., 2021; Diaz-Bonilla et al., 2023; Hasnain & Chaudhury, 2021). At least $80 billion in annual investments throughout food value chains are estimated to be required to meet the controversial 70% expected rise in food demand by 2050 (The World Bank, 2020). Observers, at least in the business community, consider the financial needs for a more sustainable future would be even higher (Nidumolu et al., 2009).

Alternative and sustainable finance schemes such as the social finance discussed earlier (see Stephens, 2021), and blended finance that mobilizes commercial banks, non-bank financial institutions, and their clients are proposed and used with varied successes (Apampa et al., 2021). For example, the convergence database of blended finance has recorded over 146 transactions targeting the agriculture sector and/or SDG 2 (Zero Hunger), amounting to $13.4 billion since 2015 (Convergence, 2021). These schemes de-risk food systems activities' financing and draw from diverse sources in an otherwise limited pool to support the implementation (Havemann et al., 2022). If explored and fitted to the alternative visions of transformation, new financing models will stir resource mobilization for sustainable futures. The private capital dependence of alternative financing may, however, lead to lack of incentives to address social and environmental concerns (Barrett et al., 2022).

Reallocating and redirecting resources from other sectors or from other unsustainable food system ventures could be a more realistic approach. For example, unsustainable agricultural subsidies could be reallocated to sustainable food system actions (von Braun et al., 2023). Though controversial, enormous resources spent on "country pet projects" in areas such as defense, especially in the developed world, could be redirected to food systems. These kinds of actions, understandably, would likely be met with stiff political and economic resistance.

4.3.4 Converting Momentum through Technological Innovations

Having described various technological (political) actions for initiating transformative changes in the technological environment in Section 4.2.4, this section discusses ways of converting the fruits of those actions into followable and acceptable sustainable options. It emphasizes mechanisms for ensuring technological changes align with sustainability while maintaining business and social viability to compete and potentially replace unsustainable regime innovations.

4.3.4.1 Alignment of Innovations with Sustainability Indicators

Alignment of innovations with sustainability indicators is needed to ensure novel technologies and ideas contribute to achieving sustainable alternative visions of food systems and to show their difference from unsustainable practices. By aligning innovations to sustainability indicators, we are referring to ensuring that novelties have sustainability as an explicit motivator (Matthews et al., 2019) and that there are readily verifiable indicator systems/frameworks to guide innovation processes. Such a process could ensure innovations truly facilitate food systems sustainability, and claims of innovation-driven sustainable food systems shifts can be easily assessed.

There are already laudable efforts to develop models and frameworks for sustainability indicators that could be leveraged to guide food systems (Aznar-Sánchez et al., 2020; Poponi et al., 2022; Silvestri et al., 2024) and possibly innovation processes. For example, the Food Sustainability Index (FSI) examines food systems performance across the three pillars of food loss and waste, sustainable agriculture, and nutritional challenges. The 38 indicators and 95 sub-indicators of the Framework address societal, environmental, and economic themes (The Economist, 2025). These types of indices lay a foundation for adaptation into the technology and innovation space. Specific to innovations, existing measures such as the Technology for Social Good indices (Tsuda et al., 2007), the Sustainable Sustainability Index (TSI, 2025), and the Technology

Readiness Level (TRL) that incorporate sustainability are proposed and variedly tested in the innovation space. These measures can be adapted to the specific context of food system innovations. Negra et al. (2020) proposed a model in which the scientific world and businesses can co-develop new indicators to provide strategic approaches for companies to integrate sustainability. Such frameworks offer essential directions for creating context-specific indicators that could be leveraged to align innovations with sustainability.

More specific indicators must be developed to align with certain lines of sustainability. For example, Silvestri et al. (2024) reviewed the literature on indicators for measuring sustainability and circular economy in the agri-food sector. They found that, though mostly incomprehensive, there are undoubtedly wide-ranging indicators in that area. They argued for an integrated approach (environmental, social, and economic) as the best solution to ensure an easier transition. Similarly, Poponi et al. (2022) reviewed the literature and identified 102 indicators, classified into 8 scopes for evaluating the transition to the circular economy in the agri-food sector. Evidently, there is no shortage of indicators to measure sustainability toward particular visions of the food systems, and such efforts will continue. However, fragmentation and lack of consensus on what should be included as indicators must be tackled to make such efforts effective for decision-making (Aramyan et al., 2006). Therefore, efforts to develop sustainability indicators that fit the context of agri-food technical innovations are needed for the proposed alignments to happen. The research community must work with the innovation and business community in this task.

It is also important to curate and present innovations aligned with sustainability in accessible ways as a means for accountability. Here, dashboards proposed by Poponi et al. (2022) and other visualization mechanisms are used to turn indicators into guides from which the innovation processes can be assessed. The effective data for implementation, monitoring, and evaluation can provide the basis for aligning innovations to sustainability (Gillespie et al., 2013).

4.3.4.2 Creating a Business Case for Innovation Using Financial Instruments

Another measure to convert alternative innovation forces into sustainable regime options is *creating a business case for innovations using financial instruments*. Undoubtedly, as discussed previously (cf Section 4.1.4), in capitalist food systems, only the fittest of innovations, technologies, and businesses survive (ETC Group, 2022; Whitfield, 2017). Using financial instruments to create business cases could open the door for sustainable alternative innovations. Once it turns out that an innovation shows promising ecological and social properties but at least temporarily lacks economic competitiveness, regulations and financial instruments that reduce risk can be used to aid their successful competition with less sustainable counterparts (Horbach, 2005). If aligned with alternative sustainable visions of food systems, emerging sustainable financial instruments such as green bonds, banks, and investment funds (Gyura, 2020; Maltais & Nykvist, 2020) may provide the needed business environment for innovations. However, choosing financial instruments must be carefully done to avoid the continued risk of innovations' financialization (Burch & Lawrence, 2009; Clapp, 2014).

In the neoliberal capitalist food system, quantifying the value (economic and financial) of sustainable innovations would compete with and displace unsustainable technologies. Efforts for true cost accounting to cater to social and environmental costs of food innovations (Baker et al., 2020; Gemmill-Herren et al., 2021; Michalke et al., 2023) are steps toward sustainability-inclined quantification of benefits. Existing methods, such as cost–benefit analysis and returns on investments of innovations that leverage true cost accounting, would be critical. The proliferation of methods for true cost accounting for food (see de Adelhart Toorop et al., 2021) could provide entry points for quantifying and creating business cases for innovations used in producing food. These methods not only show the value of sustainable food but could be used to assess the cost of unsustainable options (and their innovations) (Michalke et al., 2023) to make the business case for alternatives.

The discussion in this section emphasized how to convert new, alternative food systems into sustainable options that allow potential followers to draw from their practices. Measures are required across the four political domains of action for potential transformative novelties to come into the limelight of food systems instead of being confined to the margins of the dominant food institutions and practices.

4.4 Issues in Managing Trade-offs, Reducing Incoherence and Prioritizing Actions

Following discussions of the various resistance to change (cf Section 4.1) and actions that could create and maintain new momentum (cf Section 4.2) and convert that momentum into sustainable options (cf Section 4.3), this section will discuss the mechanisms of managing inevitable trade-offs that will emanate undertaking the previous actions. Specifically, this section builds on the critical role of managing trade-offs described in Section 3.4 to discuss specific mechanisms of this process. In describing the complexity of resistance to food systems transformation and the actions to initiate new and alternative momentum and turn those into sustainable regime options in the previous sections, we emphasized how the decisions and processes are always multifaceted and involve diverse actors. Such complexities, diversity of actors, and processes lend themselves to confusion, such as which resistance must be tackled first. Which actions should be pursued first to create new momentum or convert the momentum, and how can that be done with minimal negative consequences on vulnerable food system actors who depend on the conventional regime? Which actors must be involved in the processes of creating and converting momentum? Which sustainability visions or ideals should be pursued and embedded into alternative food system pursuits? These and many other questions bordered on uncertainties, competition, and conflicts necessitate the actions discussed in this section as mechanisms to manage trade-offs and reduce incoherence in the food system transformation process. In Table 6 and the following paragraphs, we outline some of the political actions as documented or proposed in the literature.

4.4.1 Managing Trade-offs and Prioritization through Framing, the Political Economy of Actors, Knowledge, and Evidence

This section discusses managing trade-offs and prioritization through actions of framing, the political economy of actors, knowledge, and evidence. Particularly, we set out specific mechanisms in the context of the political economy of diverse actors engaged in food system actions.

4.4.1.1 Documenting and Quantifying Trade-offs

Documenting and quantifying trade-offs is a critical step to managing the food system transformation process to ensure it yields optimal sustainability outcomes. The inherent nature of trade-offs and their implications for food systems' decision-making makes it necessary to document them at every stage of the transformation.

We are currently witnessing several efforts to develop systematic frameworks for food systems analysis (Amiri et al., 2020; Foran et al., 2014; Gaitan-Cremaschi et al., 2019; Zurek et al., 2018), which, according to Zurek et al. (2021), can increase our understanding of the complex interactions needed to identify trade-offs and facilitate synergies between alternative interventions. Methods and techniques such as trade-off analysis/anticipation, synthesis studies, visioning and backcasting, modeling tools, and foresight processes, such as trend analysis or scenario planning, have commonly been drawn for such purposes (Antle & Valdivia, 2021; Lentz, 2021; Wiebe & Prager, 2021; Zurek et al., 2021).

Table 6 Issues managing trade-offs, reducing incoherence, and prioritizing actions

Domains	The process	4. Managing trade-offs, reducing incoherence, and prioritizing actions	
		Issues	Selected references
Discursive practices / instrumental power	Framing, the political economy of actors, knowledge, and evidence	• Documenting and quantifying cross-sectoral trade-offs • Strengthening delivery of vertical coherence • Use of multi-stakeholder platforms to establish collaborative or pluralist/fragmented governance • Delivery of horizontal coherence (multisectoral coordination)	(Ambrose et al., 2022; Antle & Valdivia, 2021; Gillespie et al., 2019; Herens et al., 2022; Hubeau et al., 2017; IPES-Food, 2023; Jagustovic et al., 2021; Rutten et al., 2018; Sonnino et al., 2019; Valdivia et al., 2012; Zurek et al., 2021)
	Cultural dynamics, norms, and behavior	• Development of mechanisms of accountability of and to citizens and CSOs	(Andrée et al., 2019; Brouwer et al., 2021; FIAN International, 2020; Hassanein, 2003; IPES-Food, 2023; Kraak et al., 2014; Renting & Wiskerke, 2010; Swinburn et al., 2015)

Table 6 (cont.)

Domains	The process	4. Managing trade-offs, reducing incoherence, and prioritizing actions	
		Issues	Selected references
Institutional capacity and technology	Capacity and financial resources (of the public sector)	• Prioritization and sequencing of financing	(Augustin et al., 2021; Barrett et al., 2022; Conevska et al., 2019; Gillespie et al., 2013; Lentz, 2021; von Braun, 2009; Von Braun, 2008)
	Technological innovations	• Dis-incentivize emergence of unsustainable technological innovations	(Barrett et al., 2022; Boysen et al., 2019; Duncan et al., 2019; Figeczky et al., 2021; Hellin et al., 2020; Herrero et al., 2020; Miles et al., 2017b)

Modeling, using mathematical methods, of food systems processes, actions, and outcomes to identify trade-offs and synergies is a common approach (Antle & Valdivia, 2021; Jagustovic et al., 2021). For example, computer-assisted optimization routines or other evidence-based analytical approaches have been used to select the best solution to meet certain nutrition goals, with an active consortium developed on these processes (see https://www.nyas.org/programs/nutrition-modeling-consortium/). These models have been applied by international organizations to inform national government and stakeholder decision-making (see Knight et al., 2022). However, more advanced statistical tools are required to project and model the potential impact of different policies and actions, especially when these impacts are felt across multiple outcomes (e.g., between food security and environmental sustainability objectives).

Efforts at more comprehensive approaches to trade-off identification and documentation are also unfolding, combining multiple techniques to improve the robustness of trade-offs and synergy management. For instance, the European Union, Metrics, Models, and Foresight for European SUStainable Food and Nutrition Security (SUSFANS) developed food systems performance metrics, a modeling and visualization toolbox that helps identify and manage trade-offs and synergies. Multi-method approaches, including stakeholder engagements, the creation of a conceptual framework, performance metrics, modeling for quantifying sustainability status, and visualization to highlight outcomes and trade-offs, were the bedrock of the process (Kuiper et al., 2017; Rutten et al., 2018; Zurek et al., 2017, 2018). These experiences could be adapted and expanded across places and food systems to identify and quantify trade-offs, synergies, and prioritization of actions.

Whether through visioning, foresight, or any other form of trade-off identification, the participation of diverse stakeholders would be crucial. Participatory processes that bring together scientists and diverse actors to identify key impact indicators are encouraged. For example, laying the foundation for the ONE CGIAR system, Antle and Valdivia (2021) showed trade-off and foresight analysis of agri-food systems, as applied in East Africa Dairy Development (EADD) Project (see Valdivia et al., 2012) and The AgMIP; the Crop–Livestock Intensification Project (see Tui et al., 2021) has the potential for providing integrated assessments of economic, environmental, and social impacts at low cost and promptly. The strength of these approaches, they note, lies in their participatory processes.

It is necessary to visualize possible outcomes, pathways, and decisions and how they affect the various components. Dashboards, scorecards, indices, and profiles are common visualization typologies used in decision-making (HLPE, 2022), which would be helpful in this process. Successful examples and visualization experiences abound to learn from, especially from the nutrition field; at least 14 visualization tools were launched between 2017 and 2018 (Manorat et al., 2019). However, these tools must be improved to dynamically engage and interact with different variables to aid decision-making (Marshall et al., 2021).

4.4.1.2 Strengthening Delivery of Vertical Coherence

Key to managing trade-offs and synergies is strengthening the delivery of vertical coherence in food system governance processes. Vertical coherence entails ensuring different levels of government – international, national, regional, and local – follow common policy objectives and align food systems' actions toward established normative goals (OECD, 2015, 2016; Parsons & Hawkes, 2019). The complexity of food systems compels roles by different actors across levels, including local, regional, national, and international. Actors at each of these levels may have varying needs, objectives, and expected outcomes, which opens avenues for conflicts and contestations when those are not aligned. Likewise, certain food systems actions' spillover effects (e.g., impacts on climate and trade systems) may manifest beyond borders, necessitating international interventions (Giuseppe, 2015; OECD, 2016) that transcend one level of operations. Hence, mechanisms that ensure decision-making across these levels are reconciled are critical, especially in the context of sustainable transformation when more systemic changes are necessary.

Multilevel governance initiatives are suggested and applied to strengthen vertical coherence (Edwards et al., 2024; Marzeda-Mlynarska, 2011; OECD, 2010, 2016). Many approaches are being applied to the food system–specific drive for coherence. The creation of broad policy initiatives such as the SDGs, the European Union Farm to Fork Strategy, and diverse national-level food policies is used to provide a framework of action upon which all other levels of government draw directions (Bizikova, 2023; Edwards et al., 2024). However, in practice, weak linkages to the subnational levels are limited and have limited the operationalization of this approach in many contexts (Bizikova, 2023). Bridging organizations such as food policy councils that operate at multiple scales are also proposed and used (e.g., Canada Food Policy Council) as a way to bring different levels and sectors of food into coherent policy action (Edwards et al., 2024). The way these bridging entities are designed and the communication channels between the various levels are crucial.

How multilevel governance initiatives are structured determines their success in strengthening the delivery of vertical coherence. According to the OECD (2010), multilevel governance for positive change must be created around: (1)

participatory governance and strategic planning at the relevant scale, (2) providing an analytical foundation for short- and long-term planning, (3) encouraging experimentation and innovation, and (4) long-term planning horizon. Building capacities of agencies at both the national and subnational levels could help improve policy consistency and harmonize priorities across food system policy scales (Bizikova, 2023).

The institutional governance arrangement around these principles could enhance the coherence of food systems policies while minimizing potential trade-offs.

4.4.1.3 Use of Multi-Stakeholder Platforms to Establish Collaborative or Pluralist/Fragmented Governance

Multi-stakeholder platforms (MSPs), "governed spaces for multistakeholder interaction, bringing together multiple actors (from different sectors), involving a certain level of institutionalization" (Herens et al., 2022), have emerged as strong mechanisms for food system action. According to Thorpe et al. (2021, p. 3), the interest in MSPs is driven by "a recognition that transformation in complex systems cannot be achieved through simple or technical fixes," which are likely to have insufficient results. Instead, change requires new forms of governance that bring stakeholders, including experts, government, civil society, private sectors, and individuals, together to plan and act in new ways.

The potential governance-shaping roles of MSPs have led to their proliferation with hopes of stimulating alternative and effective food systems governance (Termeer et al., 2018). A common example of MSP is the Food Policy Councils/groups at the municipal and sometimes state level in the United States, Canada, and the United Kingdom (and emerging in other regions), with over 320 in the United States alone by 2020 (FIAN International, 2020). These entities bring together a diversity of food systems duty-bearers, rights-bearers, and other stakeholders to examine food systems in a specific region, develop recommendations, and coordinate activities for change. Such efforts could be critical for assessing food systems to agree on the best pathways for transformation. In their review of existing MSP for food systems transformation, Herens et al. (2022) identified over 89 platforms in Bangladesh, Vietnam, Ethiopia, and Nigeria – facilitated by supranational bodies, NGOs, policy, research, humanitarian, and international donors. At the regional scale, for example, the SFS-MED platform, for example, has been set up by FAO, CIHEAM, and the Union for the Mediterranean Secretariat as a multi-stakeholder initiative to provide a space where stakeholders from policy, science, and technology have dialogue in shaping sustainable food systems (Bedeau et al., 2021; Ridolfi et al., 2020).

There are concerns surrounding the prospects of these platforms. While some MSPs, such as the Scaling-up Nutrition Platform (SUN), are argued as being successful in their causes, including shifting discourses, they have been less promising in driving shifts to systems-based narratives (Herens et al., 2022). One key challenge to their effectiveness is cited as the "stakeholder" paradigm – grounded in a largely undifferentiated categorization of actors ("stakeholders") – allowing powerful corporations to dominate governance processes (IPES-Food, 2023). The hijacking of the UNFSS processes and dialogues to further corporate interest (Canfield et al., 2021b; Clapp et al., 2021; Yates et al., 2021) is a case of how platforms can be turned against the true ideals of transformation. Ultimately, in their current formation, MSPs may be less well suited to support radical change unless critical issues, including leadership, motivations, capacities, and clear guidance, are addressed (Gillespie et al., 2013; Herens et al., 2022)

Deliberate efforts to build around interactive learning, empowerment, co-creation, and participatory governance could enhance the effectiveness of MSPs (HLPE, 2017, 2020). Institutionalizing and mandating platforms, including catering to trade-offs and synergies, may as well improve effectiveness in delivering transformative change (Kugelberg et al., 2021) by minimizing turnovers associated with democratic political changes, as evidenced in nutrition modeling practices (Knight et al., 2022). Private engagement in such platforms must move beyond uncritical stakeholderism to processes of earning authentic trust through demonstrating a sustained commitment to visions of transformation (Yates et al., 2021).

4.4.1.4 Delivery of Horizontal Coherence (Multisectoral Coordination)

As has been acknowledged (HLPE, 2017; IPES-Food & ETC Group, 2021; Mattioni et al., 2022; Ruben et al., 2021; Sonnino et al., 2019; Torres-Salcido & Sanz-Canada, 2018), (horizontal) coordination among the organizations and agencies representing the many sectors in the food systems minimizes trade-offs and ensures synergies in food system governance. The food system encompasses sectors such as agriculture, health, nutrition, environment, and business, with each associated with their sector ontologies of food systems, as well as the objectives and outcomes they wish to achieve. This diversity breeds complexity of the food system challenges, processes, and outcomes and creates avenues for contentions. Hence, transformative changes in this context cannot be delivered with siloed interventions (Bedeau et al., 2021), necessitating multisectoral coordination that allows ministries to articulate their respective roles and interests so as to identify potential tensions, conflicts, trade-offs, and synergies.

Different strategies are used for the coordination and collaboration of the different food system sectors. Establishing cross-sectoral platforms used to develop and share food systems information, knowledge, and coordination expertise is an essential step. Institutionalizing platforms such as intersectoral working groups (e.g., Vietnam intersectoral technical working groups on One Health) and inter-ministerial committees (e.g., The Ethiopian Food Systems Transformation and Nutrition Inter-ministerial Steering Committee) are common approaches, especially with decentralization efforts (Gillespie et al., 2013; Rondinelli, 2017).

Broad food policies that deviate from sectorial focuses are also avenues for cross-sectorial coordination, as these policies provide a common food vision from which all sectors operate. The Canada Food Policy of 2019 is an example of this approach. The policy provided an avenue to bring previously discrete policies in agriculture, health, nutrition, Indigenous food, and others into a common shared national vision of food system change – thus bringing diverse sectors into a common umbrella (Agriculture and Agri-Food Canada, 2020). The National Pathways submitted by over 125 countries to the UNFSS process are in line with efforts to coordinate different sectors through holistic policies or policy documents. Importantly, the dialogue processes that led to these documents are shown to have facilitated cross-sectorial policy collaborations in countries such as Denmark (Remans et al., 2024).

Coordination and collaboration initiatives are essential steps to bringing different sectors of the food system together in ways that ensure consistency of policy directions and actions (Gillespie et al. 2019). Brazil's award-winning social protection program, the Bolsa Familia, is said to have been successful because of the multisectoral governance of its implementation (see Kushitor et al., 2022). Likewise, as Fanzo et al. (2020) argued, the alignment of nutrition and agricultural development and environmental sustainability, which are at an all-time high today, are consequences of multisectoral coordination. However, there is massive room for improvement across various aspects of food systems in successfully leveraging all-sector coordination to ensure the attainment of one goal does not undermine the ability to achieve other sustainability goals.

4.4.2 Managing Trade-offs and Prioritization through Cultural Dynamics, Norms, and Behavior

This section discusses how to manage trade-offs and synergies that would emerge in reshaping culture and norms for system transformation. The actions discussed here center on ways to navigate the complex politics of actors that negatively influence food system cultures and norms.

4.4.2.1 Development of Mechanisms of Accountability of and to Citizens and CSOs

Mechanisms of accountability of and to citizens and CSOs are needed to keep food system actors in check at every stage of transformation. By accountability, we refer to one actor answering to another, who is empowered to assess how well the former fulfills obligations (Andrée et al., 2019; Garton et al., 2022). It involves answering particular performance expectations (Brown et al., 2006). Establishing accountability of and to citizens and CSOs is integral to managing trade-offs and ensuring synergies. I

Mechanisms to hold food systems decision-makers, especially private actors and governments, accountable are common in the food space (Andrée et al., 2019; Hassanein, 2003; Kraak et al., 2014; Renting & Wiskerke, 2010; Swinburn et al., 2015). Corporate actors' (misuse of) power makes current food systems' accountability responses heavily focused on their activities (IPES-Food, 2023; Swinburn et al., 2015). In nutrition, the multiple accountability mechanisms emerging to hold businesses accountable for their actions have been documented and assessed (see Global Alliance for Improved Nutrition, 2019). Among the existing mechanisms, civil society leads some of the hardest in measuring performance by independently ranking companies on a wide range of nutrition-related issues, such as Access to Nutrition Index-INFORMAS. In their work on strengthening accountability for healthy diets, Swinburn et al. (2015) noted that legal (constitutional rights to food), quasi-regulatory (Codes of conduct and ethics guidelines), political (Shareholder activism), market-based (Consumer demand and boycotts), and communication (media, advocacy campaigns, opinion polls, social media, public forums, watchdog organizations, petitions, league tables, and demonstrations – cf Sections 4.2.2 and 4.2.3) are the most used measures in the food space. The campaign activities of the Corporate Accountability (https://corporateaccountability.org/food/about-our-food-campaign/) and their associated networks in the United States to hold food corporations to account for their role in unhealthy food is an example of CSO efforts in this regard.

Swinburn et al. (2015) have, however, expressed uncertainties on civil society accountability, noting that current measures are confined to public communications through media, formal channels of policy development through government committees, and invoking mechanisms to increase the transparency of government processes. These measures, though encouraging, are insufficient to address the critical concerns because they are voluntary "recommendations," "expectations," or "guidance" rather than mandatory (Swinburn et al., 2015). Even when mandatory, CSOs may lack enforcement power, legal accountability, or access to effective justice (IPES-Food, 2023). Civil society advocates have, therefore, underlined the essence of legally binding instruments, with baseline examples drawn from successful mechanisms such as the WHO Framework Convention on Tobacco Control, the WHO Framework of Engagement with Non-State Actors, and the WHO Financial Regulations and Financial Rules (IPES-Food, 2023).

Beyond CSOs, consumers have a role in food systems accountability. In theory, the most powerful lever for consumers to hold the private sector is to buy healthy, instead of unhealthy, foods (Swinburn et al., 2015), letting the demand drive the practices in what has become known as political consumerism (Boström & Micheletti, 2019; Jacobsen & Dulsrud, 2007; O'Brien & Macoun, 2022). Though less discussed, individuals, such as citizens and consumers in developing countries, have held governments and corporations accountable through purchases and protests to drive change (Hossain & Scott-Villiers, 2019; Legwegoh & Fraser, 2015). Consumer protests and riots in African capitals (Younde, Addis Ababa, Abidjan, etc.) at times of high food prices (especially during the 2007–2008 and 2010–2011 food crisis) financial crisis and resultant policy changes by some governments exemplify this form of accountability (Sneyd et al., 2013). These riots were used to voice displeasure on food prices, forcing governments to alter measures to avoid losing political support.

Developing new and strengthening older accountability measures for assessing, monitoring, and managing actors' actions is still needed. This requires agreement on public interest-based criteria for participants and strict rules mandating responsible actions. Legal mechanisms of holding accountability for CSOs and consumers must be pursued at all levels (Newell, 2008; Yates et al., 2021). Rewards must back these measures for good actions and binding sanctions for unsustainable practices.

Accountability must be a two-way process, as consumers and CSOs must also be accountable for their in-actions. Currently, many CSOs accountability is faced toward donors as they hold power to impact their activities (Brown et al., 2006). However, it is important for consumers and citizens, whom most CSOs turn to represent, to be given a voice. Different transparency mechanisms (reporting and disclosure systems), participation mechanisms (other actors involved in decision-making), evaluation mechanisms (organizational monitoring and evaluation systems, independent program evaluations, and social audits), and complaints and redress mechanisms (sanctioning) could be leveraged for CSO accountability. Mutual accountability compacts that bind CSOs, the citizens they represent, and other stakeholders interested in the food systems would facilitate shared accountabilities. Likewise, regulators of CSOs can hold them accountable to their intended values. Essentially, the type of accountability mechanism must be determined by the other actors at the other end of the issue (see Brown et al., 2006).

4.4.3 Managing Trade-offs and Prioritization through Capacity and Financial Resources (of the Public Sector)

This section describes mechanisms for managing trade-offs and prioritizing food system action in light of capacity and financial resources (of the public sector) resistance to food system change and potential complexities of decisions for creating new momentum and converting them into sustainable regime options.

4.4.3.1 Prioritization and Sequencing of Financing

All actions that remove barriers, create alternative visions, and convert them into sustainable options should ideally be implemented simultaneously. However, among many challenges, the resource and capacity constraints discussed earlier make it necessary to prioritize and sequence (Gillespie et al., 2013; Kuchiki, 2004; Von Braun, 2008). Particularly, food system transformation proposed by this Framework would entail prioritizing and sequencing actions such as which resistance to tackle first, which new sustainability action to channel scarce resources into for the most systematic change with minimal negative consequences, which innovation(s) to invest in for maximum system sustainability, and which domain of political actions to address first for broader impact.

There is no one standardized approach to prioritizing actions, as evident in governments' continuous contemplation on what to do first amid competing demands (Gillespie et al., 2013). At present, the prioritization of (food system) actions is primarily influenced by economic viability, visibility, and political gains (Timilsina, 2007; von Braun, 2010; Von Braun, 2008). This approach certainly would not deliver radical food systems transformation when we consider that some well-functioning sustainable alternatives may not always be the most visible, economically viable, or politically popular. It is, therefore, imperative to devise alternative mechanisms to prioritize food systems' actions.

Though the strategies for identifying and quantifying trade-offs and synergies discussed previously (cf Section 4.4.1) offer some foundations, more tailored and targeted methods must be developed for sustainability-oriented prioritizations. Gillespie et al. (2013) have documented one such effort developed by researchers at Harvard University and elsewhere: an economic growth diagnostics process to help government prioritization efforts. The process combines evidence about the technical (what works here?), capacity (can we scale up?), and, importantly, political (are there any windows of opportunity for change?) aspects (see Hausmann et al., 2008 for further explanation). Though a worthwhile tool to develop criteria for prioritizing and sequencing how to use limited resources, the potential lack of food context would mean further adapatation for application to food systems.

Another approach to dealing with the limited resources is bundling actions, where multiple innovations and actions are put together into packages to enhance their impact (Barrett et al., 2022). However, bundling does not answer what comes first or should be left out. Other existing methods, such as the Delphi approach and participatory prioritization tools used in the planning and project management field (see Hessami et al., 2020; Kerali & Mannisto, 1999; Wallbaum et al., 2011), could be adapted to facilitate prioritization and sequencing.

While many prioritization and sequencing tools and processes exist, each has different purposes, strengths, and limitations. To date, most tools are too broad and lack the context specificity for food systems, which makes their use somewhat ad hoc. Developing food systems-specific prioritization and sequencing tools and criteria based on individual domains, system-level outcomes, and a deeper understanding of the political economy and ethical dimensions (Horton et al., 2017) would be crucial going forward.

4.4.4 Managing Trade-offs and Prioritization through Technological Innovations

This section describes mechanisms for managing trade-offs and prioritizing food system innovation actions in processes of unblocking technological resistance to food system change, creating forces of technological innovations, and converting them into sustainable innovations in the broader food systems.

4.4.4.1 Dis-incentivize Emergence of Unsustainable Technological Innovations

Dis-incentivizing the emergence of unsustainable technological innovations is crucial to managing food systems trade-offs. This involves using instruments, processes, and actions to discourage technological innovations that do not contribute to attaining alternative sustainable visions. On multiple occasions in this Element, we have noted how current technological innovation pipelines, though argued as healthy (Herrero et al., 2020), are unsustainable, necessitating a change in direction for sustainable food systems transformation. However, it may not be enough to encourage sustainable innovations; instead, it must be complemented with disincentivizing unsustainable technologies to counter the short-term economic pull within the dominant capitalist food regime (Miles et al., 2017a).

Traditionally, similar measures of regulations, taxes, and subsidies discussed as potential incentives (cf 4.3.4) could also serve as disincentives to unsustainable technologies, if designed to have the opposite effect. The successes of sugar and beverage taxes leading some corporations to adjust behaviors in some countries (Carriedo et al., 2021; Roache & Gostin, 2017) testify to how such disincentives can influence the direction of innovations. Hence, instead of providing subsidies to unsustainable innovations like fertilizers and processed foods, ideally, higher taxes could discourage companies from continuously innovating newer unsustainable products (Food System Economics Commission, 2024). Another form of taxing used to disincentive unsustainable innovations is putting taxes or prices on practices, such as carbon taxes. The carbon tax is one of the popular forms of these taxes employed in Canada, Sweden, and the European Union to disincentive unsustainable innovations and practices, including within food systems. Research shows that when unsustainable innovations or their effects (pollution, carbon emissions) have costs associated with them, food system actors work to find ways to shift away from them to avoid the economic burden, which reduces the unsustainable outcomes (Anser et al., 2021; Habib et al., 2024). These forms of disincentives thus already exist but would need further attention in the context of food systems sustainability. More targeted and intentional disincentivizing of unstainable options is needed to ensure the private sector is not motivated to pursue them. Policy and market research to understand and devise appropriate disincentives are paramount to pursuing sustainable transformations.

It must, however, be acknowledged that placing disincentives is not a straightforward process due to the complicated position of technological innovations and the challenges in deciding what is truly sustainable. For instance, some argue sustainable technology does not exist because no one technology can meet all the metrics of sustainability (Kemp, 2010). Likewise, it is controversially argued that technologies are not inherently bad or good (Miller, 2021), but their effects are dictated by their usage. Evident in these claims is the difficulty of determining if an innovation would end up unsustainable. The development of sustainability indications could provide some foundation for overcoming this challenge.

5 Delivering Normative Food Systems Transformation through Politics – What the Framework Teaches Us

The preceding section discussed various political actions across the four processes or stages of transformation. The populated Framework of politics for the transformation of food systems is presented in Table 7, which brings the previous sections together into the holistic propositions of how to transform food systems with actions at the intersection of the domains of politics and processes/stages of transformation

The Framework posits that food systems transformation would be a process/outcome of interrelated political configurations of actions in framings, political

Table 7 Summary of the framework with domains and processes populated

Domains	The processes	Issues and challenges in:			
		1. Identifying resistance to change in the current regime	2. Creating and maintaining new momentum	3. Converting new momentum into sustainable options	4. Managing trade-offs, reducing incoherence, and prioritizing actions
Discursive practices / instrumental power	1. Framing, political economy of actors, knowledge and evidence	• Current/dominant regime coalitions' discourses – Justification (narrative) of the current status quo • Lobbying, power of influence of current incumbents (private sector) • Role of scientific paradigms and mainstream science • Economic and political interests from governments (e.g., trade export) • Dysfunctional policy-science interface and the role of media	• Framing of the problem and narratives of change (policy-makers) • Enabling and incentivizing positive contributions from the private sector • Generation of demand for evidence of effectiveness • Incentivizing of horizontal coherence (multisectoral coordination) • Advocacy to change priority (civil society)	• Translation of new framing and agenda into concrete policies • Create political coalitions in support of change • Evidence-based documentation of coverage, scale, and quality (scientific community) • Research for alternative food system configurations and 'preferred solutions'	• Documenting and quantifying cross-sectoral trade-offs • Strengthening delivery of vertical coherence • Use of multi-stakeholder platforms to establish collaborative or pluralist/fragmented governance • Delivery of horizontal coherence (multisectoral coordination)

Table 7 (cont.)

The processes / Domains		Issues and challenges in:			
		1. Identifying resistance to change in the current regime	2. Creating and maintaining new momentum	3. Converting new momentum into sustainable options	4. Managing trade-offs, reducing incoherence, and prioritizing actions
	Cultural dynamics, norms, and behavior	• Users and consumer lifestyle and values • Habitus, norms, and societal expectations	• Creating and raising consumer awareness • Building counter-narratives (civil society, users/consumers)	• Encouraging the role of civil society and individuals in changing societal values (e.g., political consumerism) • Alignment of consumer demand with food system sustainability objectives	• Development of mechanisms of accountability to citizens and CSOs
Institutional capacity and technology	Capacity and financial resources (of the public sector)	• Lack of human and/or capital resources in government institutions • Lack of know-how in government institutions	• Leadership and championing • Systemic and strategic capacity building	• Delivery and operational capacity around compliance and enforcement • Identifying new forms of resource mobilization	• Prioritization and sequencing of financing
	Technological innovation	• Absence of alternative technological solution • Technological path dependency and lock-in	• Supporting the creation and diffusion of new sustainable innovations • Creating (technological) infrastructure supporting innovations/changes	• Alignment of new innovations with food system sustainability indicators • Creating business case for innovation using financial instruments	• Dis-incentivize emergence of unsustainable technological innovations

economy of actors, knowledge and evidence, cultural dynamics, norms and behavior, capacity and financial resources (of the public sector), and technological innovation that manifest in the distinct processes of identifying resistance to change in the current regime; creating and maintaining new momentum, converting new momentum into sustainable options, and managing trade-offs, reducing incoherence, and prioritizing actions (Table 1). If well aligned, the interrelated and temporal political actions at the intersection of the domains and processes would facilitate the diagnoses of resistance and guide food systems toward sustainable transformation. Delivering food system transformation with the Framework is underscored in Section 4, with the discussions of the applied and/or proposed actions (elements) across the domains at each stage of transformation. This is incorporated into the populated Framework in Table 7, which, as we contend, is a roadmap of how to purposively leverage political actions to theoretically deliver the desired food system transformation.

The Framework identifies diverse resistance to food system change, from the individual consumer locked into social norms, habits, and culturally dictated lifestyles to large multinational corporations that leverage their financial powers to lobby governments and shape media and science. The weak financial, human, and conceptual capacities and failures of governments and the free market to produce alternative sustainable innovations also undermine transformation. Acknowledging the complexities of resistance, the Framework stipulates *creating and maintaining new momentum* through political actions such as alternative narratives (largely by civil society) that center on sustainability, leadership and championing efforts by governments and individuals, novel, decentralized processes of technological innovations, and positive incentivization of private sectors. However, alternatives created through these efforts are only as good as they are convincing enough as sustainable options.

Thus, new, alternative food systems' narratives, practices, norms, structures, and innovations must be converted into sustainable options that allow potential followers to partake. Government policies that convert alternative framing into policy actions, enhanced public sector capacity for implementation and enforcement, coalition building in support of such alternative actions, and documentation of evidence in support of the scale and successes of alternatives are crucial in this process. Without such measures, potential transformative novelties would remain confined to the margins of the dominant food institutions and practices. Across the three stages, the Framework stipulates managing trade-offs and synergies through the various actions documented or proposed in the literature, including documenting and quantifying cross-sectoral trade-offs, strengthening the delivery of vertical and horizontal coherence, use of multi-stakeholder platforms to establish collaborative or pluralist/fragmented governance, development of mechanisms of accountability to citizens and CSOs, prioritization and sequencing of financing, and dis-incentivization of unsustainable technological innovations

The Framework opens critical lessons for food system transformation. In particular, the domains and processes of the Framework, coupled with the literature-based documented political actions, extend the frontiers of our understanding of **how to (purposively) transform food systems**, especially as they relate to the foundational framework (MLP and FEEU) introduced in Section 2. We discuss three insights and lessons in the rest of this section.

5.1 The Normativity and Goal(s)-drivenness Food Systems Transformation

The first insight from the Framework is the need for normativity and directionality in food systems transformation. It emphasizes how goal(s) must be integrated into transformation processes, ensuring every step of action is guided by the desire to achieve a set outcome(s). This normativity extends the conceptual understanding of how to deliver the transitions of the MLP. The MLP conceives transformation as an outcome of interactions be niches, regimes, and landscapes, where niche innovations outside the regime also cause change when landscape pressures create windows of opportunity (cf. Section 2; Geels & Schot, 2007). The MLP process is designed with underlying assumptions of transformation as a random, given process (El Bilali, 2020). This assumption is evident in the conceptual roots of the MLP as used to describe unplanned, random transitions in energy and transport systems (Geels, 2005). This approach to systems change is extended by the Framework through its explicit normative view, intending to outline the steps necessary for a goal-directed (sustainability) food systems transformation (Ruben et al., 2021; Woodhill, 2023). This normativity is furthered through three key ways by the framework.

First, the progressive nature of four distinct processes of political actions across the four domains of politics outlined in the Framework provides the basis for normative transformation, where the steps progress toward an expected desirable end. Moving from understanding resistance to creating alternatives, converting them into sustainable options, and managing trade-offs at every point charts the direction of transformation. The processes provide directionality for change, allowing sustainable political actions and arrangements to move from overcoming resistance to having system restructuring processes, such as coalitions that transcend interests and values.

Second, visioning is an integral part of the framework that centers normativity in transformation. Visioning, which entails setting goals to pursue, is regarded as the crust of creating and maintaining new momentum in the

Framework. The Framework postulates that what makes for new and alternative momentum is the goal(s) that differs from the status quo and sets the food system toward a pathway of overcoming resistance and producing sustainable outcomes. Through these elements, the Framework anchors a goal-oriented transformation rather than random processes that some uncritically have assumed can bring the necessary change (Béné, 2022).

Finally, the ability to direct actions that deliver what we describe as multiple change mechanisms adds to the normativity of the Framework. By change mechanisms, we are referring to the mechanisms of altering nonfunctional systems, such as removing the failing pieces of the system or introducing new functional pieces. Here, the Framework integrates multiple change elements into a holistic whole. A Plethora of past and present initiatives, including, for example, the UNFSS processes for food systems transformation, turn to set a narrow focus, such as sustainable, healthy, and inclusive diets on which all actions are pitched to align (Ruben et al., 2021; van Bers et al., 2019) without explicit attention to other elements, such as resistance or ensuring alternatives maintain the path of sustainability once they are started. This approach to transformation is limiting, noncomprehensive, and shorthanded due to their potential blind spots to some change mechanisms. The persistence of the unsustainable corporate, capitalist, conventional food regimes (Holt-Giménez, 2019; IPES-Food, 2023), despite numerous efforts to destabilize them, backs our concerns and shows that a narrow focus on meeting some set goals is not enough to deliver transformations. Thus, we consider a need for directions that tackle multiple change elements holistically necessary, which the Framework has catered to through the distinct processes of political actions.

The processes outlined show how to execute food system changes that are intentional in avoiding path dependency (through identifying resistance to change), encourage novel actions that align with the desired sustainability goals (through the creation and maintaining alternative momentum and converting them into sustainable options), and explicitly cater to inevitable trade-offs in change. Thus, the Framework pushes the frontiers of transformation by simultaneously focusing on overcoming resistance, pursuing multidimensional paths of required change, aligning to desired sustainability goals, and managing trade-offs. In this sense, the framework certainly has value in spurring the normative transformation while avoiding the pitfalls of past efforts.

5.2 The Multidimensionality of Food Systems Transformation

The second insight from the Framework is the need to consider the multiple dimensions of food systems' (political) actions to deliver transformation. Political economy scholars such as Leach et al. (2020) and others (e.g., Anderson et al., 2019) have called for attention to the plurality of food systems politics to gain a fuller picture of transformation processes. Similar to the FEEU, the Framework responds to such calls through the domains of politics and their specific political actions at different stages. However, unlike the FEEU's three domains of politics (1. knowledge and evidence, 2. politics and governance, and 3. capacity and resources) the domains of politics), the Framework extends the spaces of politics to include cultural dynamics, norms, and behavior and Technological innovation. These extensions bring to light critical cultural and technological politics that the FEEU is blind to, which allows for a holistic and realistic assessment of the multidimensional politics in the food system. By acknowledging and charting out the domains that form holistic political configurations of actions in food systems, which Leach et al. (2020, p. 14) believe are necessary to achieve sustainable, equitable food systems of the future, the Framework stipulates that transformation cannot be limited to single, sector-focused solutions. Specifically, technocratic solutions alone would not transform the food systems.

The multidimensionality of food systems politics challenges current dominant approaches to food system change. Technocratic solutions such as digitalization and sustainable intensification (Barrett et al., 2022; Herrero et al., 2020; von Braun et al., 2023), favored by corporations with financial power and governments desperate for quick and visible fixes, have resulted in the political concentration on "big food" actors and innovations (Clapp & Ruder, 2020; ETC Group, 2022; IPES-Food, 2023). Though the politics of corporations and technologies are important to shaping food systems change, concentrating on those alone in search of change action risks producing half measures that do no justice to the holistic nature of transformation that current food systems require. Thus, as argued, critical considerations of politics embedded in other domains, such as capacities and resources and cultural dynamics, must be equally evaluated and actively engaged in breaking resistance and guiding change. Essentially, transforming food systems toward any specific goal – such as sustainable healthy diets – must be deliberately rooted in acknowledgments and establishment of political actions *across all the domains* demonstrated by the Framework. Such an approach opens the doors for profound and far-reaching transformations catering to food systems' multidimensional complexities and politics.

Processes that move beyond singularity to align political actions across all domains are necessary. One way to address this issue is to explore political actions through systemic, interlinked approaches. In this sense, we are suggesting and adding our voices to a growing number of scholars (Caron et al., 2018; Gill et al., 2018; HLPE, 2017; Leeuwis et al., 2021), calling for shifts to systemic, holistic, and comprehensive processes in food systems research and practice. Adopting systemic approaches allows for politics of transformations that mirror real-world processes of complexities of food systems. Such an approach adds value to isolated approaches of politics and/or transition proposed or applied in transformation.

5.3 From Enabling to a Normative Driving Environment for the Governance of Food Systems Transformation

The third and final insight from the need for creating a driving (or what some call enabling) environment for governance of food systems. Enabling environment, described as changes in more distal factors related to food systems' broad economic, political, environmental, social, and cultural context (Kampman et al., 2017; Nisbett et al., 2014), has gained prominence in the development world (Ajieroh et al., 2023; Gillespie et al., 2013; Van Den Bold et al., 2015). The concept is, however, uncritically positioned as that overreaching element on which all positive change could emerge. Though relevant to delivering some positive food system outcomes (Kampman et al., 2017), the current postulation of the enabling environment remains passive because it favors multi-stakeholder approaches without being critical of who the stakeholders are or their roles in creating the challenges that have necessitated a change in the first place. Essentially, for example, it offers limited perspectives on the private sector's role, thus allowing them to participate in the change process without actually challenging their role in perpetuating the challenges. Hence, in setting out some of the critical elements needed for Great Food Transformation, Béné (2022), one of the co-authors of this Element, called for the "establishment of not just an enabling but a normative environment." The Framework backs this proposition and begins to contemplate how to create that environment, which we describe as a driving environment.

Drawing from Gillespie et al. (2013), we define the normative driving environment for food system transformation as political processes and actions of diverse actors that aid in identifying and unlocking resistance to change, creating and maintaining momentum, turning alternatives into sustainable options, and managing trade-offs, synergies, and prioritizing action to direct pathways toward specific desirable food systems outcomes. The driving environment, as proposed by the Framework, sets the foundation for transforming the governance mechanisms of food systems. That is, the reconstitution of the "architecture of food systems" (Berry, 2019) in how formal and informal interactions between actors shape decision-making and activities (van Bers et al., 2016) related to the transformation.

The driving environment emphasizes that normative transformation is predicated on challenging how things have been governed. The diverse politics and political actions of the Framework challenge notions that transformation cannot happen without the private sector leading or being a central stakeholder (Folke et al., 2019; von Braun et al., 2023). Instead, it emphasizes governance through healthy interactions and leadership of multi-actors of the food system, including governments, consumers, civil societies, and the scientific communities. Also important in the driving environment is the movement beyond mere participation of the multi-stakeholderism; it emphasizes accountability of and to the diverse actors who have critical roles in food systems change. Through the four stages of transformation, the Framework shows what changes in institutional, policy, legal, and regulatory environments must come together for food system transformation and how those could be achieved through deliberate political actions of governments, private sectors, civil society, and consumers.

Rather than wait for political will to emerge from governments by chance or for private entities with the resource power to dictate the process, cultivating and nurturing transformation through inter-actions of all relevant actors is where the driving environment emerges. The political actions that make clear the (re)structuring of *actors' roles and interactions*, mechanisms for diverse participation, and accountability in food systems come under focus as areas of transforming governance processes. Throughout the transformation processes outlined in the Framework, multiple actors are shown to (potentially) exert power and influence in resisting, initiating, sustaining, or scaling normative change, as well as managing conflicts related to food systems' actions and outcomes. Likewise, trade-offs and synergies (of interests, values, goals, actions, and so on) abound at each stage of the transformation process. In this sense, goal-oriented governance mechanisms, different from current arrangements centered on corporate profits and productivity, are proposed for transformation. These new governance mechanisms must draw on sustainability as the basis of relationships and interactions to enhance their chances of success.

6 Concluding Reflections

Global food systems face unprecedented challenges (Dury et al., 2019; Fan et al., 2021; Haddad et al., 2016) that put attaining the Agenda 2030 and the SDGs at risk. Guidance on how to steer food systems away from unsustainable and unjust trajectories toward desirable healthy, sustainable, resilient, and equitable outcomes cannot be more timely and urgent. The setting into motion of the UNFSS process, the desperation of actors on operationalizing pathways, and the contemplations on moving from the documents to actions and eventual outcomes (UN Food Systems Coordination Hub, 2024) underscore a need for theoretical and practical guidance in delivering food systems transformation. Through this work, we make the case that food systems transformation is not an impossible goal to aspire for; however, whether we achieve any form of transformation is essentially down to how food systems politics are enacted. Politics, we posit, is at the center of creating and maintaining current unsustainable food system trajectories and shaping change processes toward sustainable goals. We expand on this argument while also taking essential steps to show how political actions could be leveraged to unlock food systems resistance and propel normative transformation by elaborating a framework.

The framework integrates multiple theoretical perspectives and practical experiences from political economy, transition, transformation, and related fields to center politics within an adaptable diagnostic and prescriptive tool for food systems transformation. As a diagnostic tool, the framework can be leveraged by diverse actors in positions to understand food system change processes. It can also be applied to understand past transformation processes and why new ideas, institutions, innovations, and narratives failed to emerge or scale up solutions. As a normative, prescriptive tool, the political actions and stages outlined provide guides and steps to assess and direct transformation interventions internationally, nationally, and at subnational scales. However, the framework is not limited to delivering food systems transformation; it can be adapted to assess and design political actions specific to particular normative goals, such as healthy, sustainable diets, undernutrition reduction, obesity reduction, and food insecurity, and for specific contexts.

Cognizant of the need for context-specific and place-based solutions (Ambikapathi et al., 2022; Caron et al., 2018), this is not a universal prescription; instead, we view the Framework as an adaptable tool. We have only used the global food systems as the arena to illustrate the politics that (could) play out at each stage of transformation. The nature of politics may vary across typologies of food systems (traditional, modern, consolidating), levels of development, or scales of consideration (international, national, subnational, and community). We suggest drawing on specific politics of framings, cultures, public capacities, and innovations as they manifest within different contexts – to diagnose and propose place-context-system-specific political actions for food systems transformation. Table 8 provides some broad guiding questions for applying the Framework in identifying current or potential political configurations of action for transformation. These sample questions are only guides to the kind of insights change makers could leverage the Framework to reveal in their food system transformation processes; hence, they can be adapted and extended based on context.

Table 8 Sample guiding questions of practical and contextual adaptation of the Framework

The domains	The processes	Issues and challenges in:		
		1. Identifying resistance to change in the current regime	2. Creating and maintaining new momentum	3. Converting new momentum into sustainable options
Discursive practices / instrumental power	Framing, political economy of actors, knowledge, and evidence	Who are the current dominant actors in the food system, and what narratives are driving their actions? What activities or strategies are dominant actors using to consolidate power and perpetuate their interest?	How can policy actors reframe the problem of food system to capture the root problem and inform alternative interventions? How can private sector be incentivized to change behaviors and chart more sustainable paths?	How can alternative new framing and agenda into be translated into concrete policies? What political coalitions of change exist or can be created to support of change? How research be used to support preferred solutions?
	Cultural dynamics, norms, and behaviors	What are the longstanding or emerging unsustainable food practices? What are the cultural norms and habits that have locked people into the unsustainable food practices?	What alternative narratives for sustainability exist or can be generated to change the directions of food systems? What forms of advocacy or communication can be used to effectively propagate alternative practices?	How can consumer demand be aligned with food system sustainability objectives and what roles can civil society play in shaping consumer behaviors?

Institutional capacity and technology	Capacity and financial resources (of the public sector)	What are the capacity gaps (of any form) of public institutions for instituting change in food system? What institutional, organizational, and conceptional limitations have locked public entities in conventional regime policies?	What mechanisms can be used to develop the capacity of leaders toward sustainability? What strategic and systemic capacities should be enhanced? What new capacities are available or must be created to support sustainability actions?	How can the operational capacity around compliance and enforcement of public institutions be enhanced to support sustainability goals?
	Technological innovation	What are the main technological innovations anchoring unsustainable food practice?	What new sustainable innovations should be created to offer competition for unsustainable technologies, and how should be created, and by who? What (technological) infrastructure exist or should be created to support alternative innovations/changes	What financial instruments exist or should be created to make business case for sustainable innovations?

Table 8 (cont.)

4. Managing trade-offs, reducing incoherence, and prioritizing actions
What innovations, behaviors, or capacities are complementary or conflicting in the process of sustainable changes in the food system? What mechanisms or institutions exists in the system for identifying and managing trade-offs? What mechanisms exist for diverse food system actors to engage in healthy ways to reconcile diverging goals and expected outcomes? What mechanisms exist for holding different actors accountable for their actions?

Moving forward, the framework would benefit from context-based empirical testing and applications to assess the feasibility of delivering normative transformations. In-depth country-level and subnational case studies are required to identify the political processes necessary for normative transformations. Through such explorations, we hope to understand the practicality of the framework in different settings to see areas for further improvements. Also, we welcome research that assesses the framework's compatibility with topic-specific theories critical for transformation, such as systems thinking, gender theories, and socio-nature.

List of Abbreviations

AgMIP	Agricultural Model Intercomparison and Improvement Project
ANVISA	National Sanitary Surveillance Agency
CAP	European Common Agriculture Policy
CFSC	Community Food Security Coalition
CGIAR	Consultative Group on International Agricultural Research
CIHEAM	Centre International de Hautes études agronomiques méditerranéennes
CSOs	Civil Society Organizations
EADD	East Africa Dairy Development
ERF	European Risk Forum
ETC	Action Group on Erosion, Technology, and Concentration
FAO	Food and Agriculture Organization of the United Nations
FEEU	Framework for the Creation of an Enabling Environment for Accelerated Undernutrition Reduction
FIAN	Food First Information and Action Network
GDP	Gross domestic product
GHG	Greenhouse gas
GIEE	Economic and Environmental Interest Group
GM	Genetically Modified
GMO	Genetically Modified Organism
HLPE	High Level Panel of Experts on Food Security and Nutrition
HLEG	High-Level Expert Group
IPBES	Intergovernmental Science-Policy Platform on Biodiversity and Ecosystem Services
IPES	International Panel of Experts on Sustainable Food Systems
LMIC	Low- and Middle-income Countries
MLP	Multi-level Perspectives of transition
MSPs	Multi-stakeholder platforms
NCDs	Noncommunicable diseases
NSBCC	Nutrition Social Behavior Change Communication
OECD	Organisation for Economic Co-operation and Development
PFP	People's Food Policy
R&D	Research and development
SDG	Sustainable Development Goals
SFS-MED	Sustainable Food Systems in the Mediterranean
S-LCA	Social Life Cycle Assessment

SPIs	Science-Policy Interface(s)
STPI	Sustainable Technology Performance Index
SUN	Scaling-up Nutrition Platform
SUSFANS	European Union, Metrics, Models, and Foresight for European SUStainable Food and Nutrition Security
TRL	Technology Readiness Level
UN	United Nations
UNFSS	United Nations Food Systems Summit,
USDA	United States Department of Agriculture
WHO	World Health Organization

References

Abdulai, A.-R. (2022). A new green revolution (GR) or neoliberal entrenchment in agri-food systems? Exploring narratives around digital agriculture (DA), food systems, and development in sub-Sahara Africa. *The Journal of Development Studies*, 58(8), 1588–1604. https://doi.org/10.1080/00220388.2022.2032673.

Abdulai, A.-R., Krishna Bahadur, KC, & Fraser, E. (2022). What factors influence the likelihood of rural farmer participation in digital agricultural services? Experience from smallholder digitalization in Northern Ghana. *Outlook on Agriculture*, 52(1), 57–66. https://doi.org/10.1177/00307270 221144641.

Acton, R. B., & Hammond, D. (2020). Impact of sugar taxes and front-of-package nutrition labels on purchases of protein, calcium and fibre. *Preventive Medicine*, 136, 106091. https://doi.org/10.1016/j.ypmed.2020.106091.

Acton, R. B., Jones, A. C., Kirkpatrick, S. I., Roberto, C. A., & Hammond, D. (2019). Taxes and front-of-package labels improve the healthiness of beverage and snack purchases: A randomized experimental marketplace. *International Journal of Behavioral Nutrition and Physical Activity*, 16(1), 46. https://doi.org/10.1186/s12966-019-0799-0.

Agriculture and Agri-Food Canada. (2020). The Food Policy for Canada [Program-service description]. https://agriculture.canada.ca/en/department/initiatives/food-policy-canada.

Ajates Gonzalez, R., Thomas, J., & Chang, M. (2018). Translating agroecology into policy: The case of France and the United Kingdom. *Sustainability*, 10(8), 2930. https://doi.org/10.3390/su10082930.

Ajates, R. (2022). From land enclosures to lab enclosures: Digital sequence information, cultivated biodiversity and the movement for open source seed systems. *The Journal of Peasant Studies*, 50(3), 1056–1084. https://doi.org/10.1080/03066150.2022.2121648.

Ajieroh, V., Onabolu, A., Ezekannagha, O., & Adeyemi, O. (2023). Fostering an enabling environment for nutrition-sensitive agriculture and food systems in Nigeria. *Food and Nutrition Bulletin*, 44(1_suppl), S3–S13. https://doi.org/10.1177/03795721231173852.

Aldrovandi, S., Brown, G. D. A., & Wood, A. M. (2015). Social norms and rank-based nudging: Changing willingness to pay for healthy food. *Journal of Experimental Psychology: Applied*, 21(3), 242–254. https://doi.org/10.1037/xap0000048.

References

Allen, P., & Guthman, J. (2006). From "old school" to "farm-to-school": Neoliberalization from the ground up. *Agriculture and Human Values*, 23(4), 401–415. https://doi.org/10.1007/s10460-006-9019-z.

Almiron, N., & Zoppeddu, M. (2015). Eating meat and climate change: The media blind spot – A study of Spanish and Italian press coverage. *Environmental Communication*, 9(3), 307–325. https://doi.org/10.1080/17524032.2014.953968.

Alroe, H. F., Moller, H., Laessoe, J., & Noe, E. (2016). Opportunities and challenges for multicriteria assessment of food system sustainability. *Ecology and Society*, 21(1), 38. https://doi.org/10.5751/ES-08394-210138.

Altieri, M. A. (Ed.). (1995). *Agroecology: The Science of Sustainable Agriculture* (2nd ed.). Westview Press.

Amadi, L., & Ekekwe, E. (2014). Corruption and development administration in Africa: Institutional approach. *African Journal of Political Science and International Relations*, 8(6), 163.

Ambikapathi, R., Schneider, K. R., Davis, B., et al. (2022). Global food systems transitions have enabled affordable diets but had less favourable outcomes for nutrition, environmental health, inclusion and equity. *Nature Food*, 3(9), 764–779. https://doi.org/10.1038/s43016-022-00588-7.

Ambrose, G., Siddiki, S., & Brady, U. (2022). Collaborative governance design in local food systems in the United States. *Policy Design and Practice*, 5(3), 362–383. https://doi.org/10.1080/25741292.2022.2109253.

Amiri, A., Mehrjerdi, Y. Z., Jalalimanesh, A., & Sadegheih, A. (2020). Food system sustainability investigation using system dynamics approach. *Journal of Cleaner Production*, 277, 124040. https://doi.org/10.1016/j.jclepro.2020.124040.

Anderson, C. R., Bruil, J., Chappell, M. J., Kiss, C., & Pimbert, M. P. (2019). From transition to domains of transformation: Getting to sustainable and just food systems through agroecology. *Sustainability*, 11(19), 5272. https://doi.org/10.3390/su11195272.

Anderson, M. (2019). The importance of vision in food system transformation. *Journal of Agriculture, Food Systems, and Community Development*, 9(A), Article A. https://doi.org/10.5304/jafscd.2019.09A.001.

Anderson, M. D., & Rivera-Ferre, M. (2021). Food system narratives to end hunger: Extractive versus regenerative. *Current Opinion in Environmental Sustainability*, 49, 18–25. https://doi.org/10.1016/j.cosust.2020.12.002.

Anderson, M., & Leach, M. (2019). Transforming food systems: The potential of engaged political economy. *IDS Bulletin*, 50(2), Article 2. https://doi.org/10.19088/1968-2019.123.

References

Anderson, M., Nisbett, N., Clément, C., & Harris, J. (2019). Introduction: Valuing different perspectives on power in the food system. *IDS Bulletin*, 50(2), 1–12. https://doi.org/10.19088/1968-2019.114.

Andrée, P., Clark, J. K., Levkoe, C. Z., & Lowitt, K. (2019). Introduction – Traversing theory and practice: Social movement engagement in food systems governance for sustainability, justice, and democracy. In Andre et al. (eds.), *Civil Society and Social Movements in Food System Governance* (pp. 1–18). () Routledge.

Andreyeva, T., Long, M. W., & Brownell, K. D. (2010). The impact of food prices on consumption: A systematic review of research on the price elasticity of demand for food. *American Journal of Public Health*, 100(2), 216–222. https://doi.org/10.2105/AJPH.2008.151415.

Anser, M. K., Khan, M. A., Nassani, A. A., et al. (2021). Relationship of environment with technological innovation, carbon pricing, renewable energy, and global food production. *Economics of Innovation and New Technology*, 30(8), 807–842. https://doi.org/10.1080/10438599.2020.1787000.

Antle, J. M., & Valdivia, R. O. (2021). Trade-off analysis of agri-food systems for sustainable research and development. *Q Open*, 1(1), qoaa005. https://doi.org/10.1093/qopen/qoaa005.

Apampa, A., Clubb, C., Cosgrove, B. E., et al. (2021). Scaling up critical finance for sustainable food systems through blended finance. Discussion Paper. CGIAR Research Program on Climate Change, Agriculture and Food Security (CCAFS). https://cgspace.cgiar.org/server/api/core/bitstreams/4b8dbd37-b2f4-4a79-b87b-271fe09bb701/content

Aramyan, L. H., Beekman, G., Galama, J., et al. (2021). Moving from niche to norm: Lessons from food waste initiatives. *Sustainability*, 13(14), 7667. https://doi.org/10.3390/su13147667.

Aramyan, L., Ondersteijn, C. J. M., Kooten, O. V., & Lansink, A. O. (2006). Performance indicators in agri-food production chains. *Frontis*, 15, 47–64. https://library.wur.nl/ojs/index.php/frontis/article/view/1141.

Araújo, K. (2014). The emerging field of energy transitions: Progress, challenges, and opportunities. *Energy Research & Social Science*, 1, 112–121. https://doi.org/10.1016/j.erss.2014.03.002.

Asamane, E. A., Marinda, P. A., Khayeka-Wandabwa, C., & Powers, H. J. (2021). Nutritional and social contribution of meat in diets: Interplays among young urban and rural men. *Appetite*, 156, 104959. https://doi.org/10.1016/j.appet.2020.104959.

Augustin, M. A., Cole, M. B., Ferguson, D., Hazell, N. J. G., & Morle, P. (2021). Perspective article: Towards a new venture science model for transforming food systems. *Global Food Security*, 28, 100481. https://doi.org/10.1016/j.gfs.2020.100481.

Avelino, F., & Wittmayer, J. M. (2016). Shifting power relations in sustainability transitions: A multi-actor perspective. *Journal of Environmental Policy and Planning*, 18(5), 628–649. Scopus. https://doi.org/10/gfvh7j.

Azevedo, A. B. C. de, Bandoni, D. H., Amorim, A. L. B. de, & Canella, D. S. (2023). Evaluation of food purchasing in the Brazilian School Feeding Programme: Feasibility of the requirements and recommendations. *Public Health Nutrition*, 26(12), 3331–3342. https://doi.org/10.1017/S136898002300229X.

Aznar-Sánchez, J. A., Mendoza, J. M. F., Ingrao, C., et al. (2020). Indicators for circular economy in the agri-food sector. *Resources Conservation Recycling*, 163, 105028.

Azuike, E. C., Emelumadu, O. F., Adinma, E. D., et al. (2011). Nutrition transition in developing countries: A review. *Afrimedic Journal*, 2(2), 1–5.

Babu, S. (2020). As policy makers call for building capacity for food system transformation, who is listening? | IFPRI : International Food Policy Research Institute. www.ifpri.org/blog/policy-makers-call-building-capacity-food-system-transformation-who-listening.

Bain, J. S. (1954). Economies of scale, concentration, and the condition of entry in twenty manufacturing industries. *The American Economic Review*, 44(1), 15–39.

Baker, L., Castilleja, G., De Groot Ruiz, A., & Jones, A. (2020). Prospects for the true cost accounting of food systems. *Nature Food*, 1(12), 765–767. https://doi.org/10.1038/s43016-020-00193-6.

Baker, P., & Friel, S. (2016). Food systems transformations, ultra-processed food markets and the nutrition transition in Asia. *Globalization and Health*, 12(1), Article 1. https://doi.org/10.1186/s12992-016-0223-3.

Baker, P., Lacy-Nichols, J., Williams, O., & Labonté, R. (2021). The political economy of healthy and sustainable food systems: An introduction to a special issue. *International Journal of Health Policy and Management*, 10(12), 734–744. https://doi.org/10.34172/ijhpm.2021.156.

Baker, P., Machado, P., Santos, T., et al. (2020). Ultra-processed foods and the nutrition transition: Global, regional and national trends, food systems transformations and political economy drivers. *Obesity Reviews*, 21(12), e13126. https://doi.org/10.1111/obr.13126.

Baker, P., Russ, K., Kang, M., et al. (2021). Globalization, first-foods systems transformations and corporate power: A synthesis of literature and data on the market and political practices of the transnational baby food industry. *Globalization and Health*, 17(1), 58. https://doi.org/10.1186/s12992-021-00708-1.

Barling, D., Lang, T., & Caraher, M. (2002). Joined-up food policy? The trials of governance, public policy and the food system. *Social Policy & Administration*, 36(6), 556–574. https://doi.org/10.1111/1467-9515.t01-1-00304.

Barrett, C. B., Benton, T., Fanzo, J., et al. (2022). *Socio-Technical Innovation Bundles for Agri-Food Systems Transformation*. Springer. https://doi.org/10.1007/978-3-030-88802-2.

Barrett, H., & Rose, D. C. (2020). Perceptions of the fourth agricultural revolution: What's in, what's out, and what consequences are anticipated? *Sociologia Ruralis*, 62(2), 162–189. https://doi.org/10.1111/soru.12324.

Barry, A. (2002). The anti-political economy. *Economy and Society*, 31(2), 268–284. https://doi.org/10.1080/03085140220123162.

Bates, J. (2014). The strategic importance of information policy for the contemporary neoliberal state: The case of Open Government Data in the United Kingdom. *Government Information Quarterly*, 31(3), 388–395.

Bear, C., & Holloway, L. (2015). Country life: Agricultural technologies and the emergence of new rural subjectivities. *Geography Compass*, 9(6), 303–315. https://doi.org/10/ggt3wx.

Bedeau, J. V., Rezaei, M., Pera, M., & Morrison, J. (2021). Towards food systems transformation in the Mediterranean region: Unleashing the power of data, policy, investment and innovation. *New Medit: Mediterranean Journal of Economics, Agriculture and Environment/Revue Méditerranéenne d'Economie Agriculture et Environment*, 20(3), 5–16.

Béné, C. (2022). Why the great food transformation may not happen – A deep-dive into our food systems' political economy, controversies and politics of evidence. *World Development*, 154, 105881. https://doi.org/10.1016/j.worlddev.2022.105881.

Béné, C., Fanzo, J., Haddad, L., et al. (2020). Five priorities to operationalize the EAT – Lancet Commission report. *Nature Food*, 1(8), 457–459. https://doi.org/10.1038/s43016-020-0136-4.

Béné, C., & Lundy, M. (2023). Political economy of protein transition: Battles of power, framings and narratives around a false wicked problem. *Frontiers in Sustainability*, 4, 1–12. https://doi.org/10.3389/frsus.2023.1098011.

Béné, C., Oosterveer, P., Lamotte, L., et al. (2019). When food systems meet sustainability – Current narratives and implications for actions. *World Development*, 113, 116–130. https://doi.org/10.1016/j.worlddev.2018.08.011.

Berger, V. (2019). Social norm-based gamification to promote eco-friendly food choice. *Journal of Consumer Marketing*, 36(5), 666–676. https://doi.org/10.1108/JCM-01-2018-2547.

Bergh, J. C. J. M. van den, & Bruinsma, F. R. (2008). *Managing the Transition to Renewable Energy: Theory and Practice from Local, Regional and Macro Perspectives*. Edward Elgar.

Berman, E. (2011). Promoting food security: The community food security coalition. *Journal of Agricultural & Food Information*, 12(3–4), 221–231. https://doi.org/10.1080/10496505.2011.611064.

Berry, E. M. (2019). Sustainable food systems and the Mediterranean diet. *Nutrients*, 11(9), 2229.

Berti, P. R., Krasevec, J., & FitzGerald, S. (2004). A review of the effectiveness of agriculture interventions in improving nutrition outcomes. *Public Health Nutrition*, 7(5), 599–609. https://doi.org/10/cnp9nr.

Bhatia, K., & Ghanem, H. (2019). Resource mobilization for agriculture and food security. In *Sustainable Food and Agriculture* (pp. 523–541). Elsevier.

Bhutta, Z. A., Das, J. K., Rizvi, A., et al. (2013). Evidence-based interventions for improvement of maternal and child nutrition: What can be done and at what cost? *The Lancet*, 382(9890), 452–477. https://doi.org/10/f2mhzb.

Bifulco, L. (2016). *Social Policies and Public Action*. Taylor & Francis.

Birner, R., Daum, T., & Pray, C. (2021). Who drives the digital revolution in agriculture? A review of supply-side trends, players and challenges. *Applied Economic Perspectives and Policy*, 43(4), 1260–1285. https://doi.org/10/gkfkh4.

Bizikova, L. (2023). Policy Coherence and Food Systems Transformation. International Institute for Sustainable Development. www.iisd.org/articles/policy-analysis/policy-coherence-and-food-systems-transformation.

Blay-Palmer, A., Santini, G., Dubbeling, M., et al. (2018). Validating the city region food system approach: Enacting inclusive, transformational city region food systems. *Sustainability*, 10(5), 1680. https://doi.org/10.3390/su10051680.

Blay-Palmer, A., Sonnino, R., & Custot, J. (2016). A food politics of the possible? Growing sustainable food systems through networks of knowledge. *Agriculture and Human Values*, 33(1), 27–43. https://doi.org/10.1007/s10460-015-9592-0.

Bonfert, B. (2022). "What we'd like is a CSA in every town." Scaling community supported agriculture across the UK. *Journal of Rural Studies*, 94, 499–508. https://doi.org/10.1016/j.jrurstud.2022.07.013.

Bornmann, L., Haunschild, R., & Mutz, R. (2021). Growth rates of modern science: A latent piecewise growth curve approach to model publication numbers from established and new literature databases. *Humanities and Social Sciences Communications*, 8(1), Article 1. https://doi.org/10.1057/s41599-021-00903-w.

Börzel, T. A., & Risse, T. (2019). Grand theories of integration and the challenges of comparative regionalism. *Journal of European Public Policy*, 26(8), 1231–1252. https://doi.org/10.1080/13501763.2019.1622589.

Boström, M., & Micheletti, M. (2019). *The Oxford Handbook of Political Consumerism*. Oxford University Press.

Boykoff, M. T. (2008a). Lost in translation? United States television news coverage of anthropogenic climate change, 1995–2004. *Climatic Change*, 86(1–2), 1–11. https://doi.org/10.1007/s10584-007-9299-3.

Boykoff, M. T. (2008b). Media and scientific communication: A case of climate change. *Geological Society, London, Special Publications*, 305(1), 11–18. https://doi.org/10.1144/SP305.3.

Boysen, O., Boysen-Urban, K., Bradford, H., & Balié, J. (2019). Taxing highly processed foods: What could be the impacts on obesity and underweight in sub-Saharan Africa? *World Development*, 119, 55–67. https://doi.org/10.1016/j.worlddev.2019.03.006.

Boza, S., Guerrero, M., Barreda, R., & Espinoza, M. (2017). Recent Changes in Food Labelling Regulations in Latin America: The Cases of Chile and Peru. SECO Working Paper Series, SECO, World Trade Institute. https://boris.unibe.ch/id/eprint/97898

Bremmer, B., & Bos, B. (2017). Creating Niches by Applying Reflexive Interactive Design. AgroEcological Transitions. Wageningen University & Research, Wageningen.

Bronson, K., & Sengers, P. (2022). Big tech meets big ag: Diversifying epistemologies of data and power. *Science as Culture*, 31(1), 15–28. https://doi.org/10.1080/09505431.2021.1986692.

Brouwer, I. D., van Liere, M. J., de Brauw, A., et al. (2021). Reverse thinking: Taking a healthy diet perspective towards food systems transformations. *Food Security*, 13(6), 1497–1523. https://doi.org/10.1007/s12571-021-01204-5.

Brown, K. A., Timotijevic, L., Barnett, J., et al. (2011). A review of consumer awareness, understanding and use of food-based dietary guidelines. *British Journal of Nutrition*, 106(1), 15–26. https://doi.org/10.1017/S0007114511000250.

Brown, L. D., Jagadananda, L., & CIVICUS (Association). (2006). Civil Society Legitimacy and Accountability: Issues and Challenges. Hauser Center for Nonprofit Organizations, Harvard University.

Bui, S., Cardona, A., Lamine, C., & Cerf, M. (2016). Sustainability transitions: Insights on processes of niche-regime interaction and regime reconfiguration in agri-food systems. *Journal of Rural Studies*, 48, 92–103. https://doi.org/10.1016/j.jrurstud.2016.10.003.

Burch, D., & Lawrence, G. (2009). Towards a third food regime: Behind the transformation. *Agriculture and Human Values*, 26(4), 267–279. https://doi.org/10/btgj69.

Calo, A., McKee, A., Perrin, C., et al. (2021). Achieving food system resilience requires challenging dominant land property regimes. *Frontiers in Sustainable Food Systems*, 5, 1–6. https://doi.org/10.3389/fsufs.2021.683544.

Canfield, M., Anderson, M. D., & McMichael, P. (2021a). UN food systems summit 2021: Dismantling democracy and resetting corporate control of food systems. *Frontiers in Sustainable Food Systems*, 5, 661552. https://doi.org/10.3389/fsufs.2021.661552.

Canfield, M., Anderson, M. D., & McMichael, P. (2021b). UN food systems summit 2021: Dismantling democracy and resetting corporate control of food systems. *Frontiers in Sustainable Food Systems*, 5, 661552. https://doi.org/10.3389/fsufs.2021.661552.

Carolan, M. (2017). Publicising food: Big data, precision agriculture, and co-experimental techniques of addition. *Sociologia Ruralis*, 57(2), 135–154. https://doi.org/10/ggnjcv.

Carolan, M. (2018a). "Smart" farming techniques as political ontology: Access, sovereignty and the performance of neoliberal and not-so-neoliberal worlds. *Sociologia Ruralis*, 58(4), 745–764. https://doi.org/10/gfgk23.

Carolan, M. (2018b). *The Real Cost of Cheap Food*. Routledge. https://doi.org/10.4324/9781315113234.

Carolan, M. (2020). Digitization as politics: Smart farming through the lens of weak and strong data. *Journal of Rural Studies*, 91, 208–216. https://doi.org/10.1016/j.jrurstud.2020.10.040.

Carolan, M. S. (2013). *Reclaiming Food Security*. Routledge. https://doi.org/10.4324/9780203387931.

Caron, P., Ferrero y de Loma-Osorio, G., Nabarro, D., et al. (2018). Food systems for sustainable development: Proposals for a profound four-part transformation. *Agronomy for Sustainable Development*, 38(4), 41. https://doi.org/10.1007/s13593-018-0519-1.

Carriedo, A., Koon, A. D., Encarnación, L. M., et al. (2021). The political economy of sugar-sweetened beverage taxation in Latin America: Lessons from Mexico, Chile and Colombia. *Globalization and Health*, 17(1), Article 1. https://doi.org/10.1186/s12992-020-00656-2.

Carriedo, A., Walls, H., & Brown, K. A. (2022). Acknowledge the elephant in the room: The role of power dynamics in transforming food systems; Comment on "what opportunities exist for making the food supply nutrition friendly? A policy space analysis in Mexico." *International Journal of*

Health Policy and Management, 11(12), 3137. https://doi.org/10.34172/ijhpm.2022.7382.

Centre for Responsible Politics, Street, NW, & Washington, S. 800. (2022). Agribusiness Lobbying Profile. OpenSecrets. www.opensecrets.org/federal-lobbying/sectors/summary?cycle=2022&id=A.

Claeys, P. (2013). From Food Sovereignty to Peasants' Rights: An Overview of Via Campesina's Struggle for New Human Rights. *La Via Campesina's Open Book: Celebrating 20 Years of Struggle and Hope*. https://www.viacampesina.org/en/wp-content/uploads/sites/2/2013/05/EN-02.pdf

Clancy, K., & Ruhf, K. (2010). Is local enough? Some arguments for regional food systems. *Choices*, 25(1), 1–5.

Clapp, J. (2014). Financialization, distance and global food politics. *The Journal of Peasant Studies*, 41(5), 797–814. https://doi.org/10/ggt3kj.

Clapp, J. (2021). The problem with growing corporate concentration and power in the global food system. *Nature Food*, 2(6), Article 6. https://doi.org/10.1038/s43016-021-00297-7.

Clapp, J., Noyes, I., & Grant, Z. (2021). The food systems summit's failure to address corporate power. *Development*, 64(3), 192–198. https://doi.org/10.1057/s41301-021-00303-2.

Clapp, J., & Ruder, S.-L. (2020). Precision technologies for agriculture: Digital farming, gene-edited crops, and the politics of sustainability. *Global Environmental Politics*, 20(3), 49–69. https://doi.org/10/ghfnq9.

Clark, J. K., Lowitt, K., Levkoe, C. Z., & Andree, P. (2021). The power to convene: Making sense of the power of food movement organizations in governance processes in the Global North. *Agriculture and Human Values*, 38(1), 175–191. https://doi.org/10.1007/s10460-020-10146-1.

Clayton, A., Oakley, P., & Taylor, J. (2000). Civil Society Organizations and Service Provision (Issue 2). United Nations Research Institute for Social Development Geneva.

Clément, C. W.-Y. (2019). Hybrid governance as rural development: Market, state, and civil society in Correns, France. In Andrée, Peter et al. (Eds.), *Civil Society and Social Movements in Food System Governance*(pp. 183–200). Routledge.

Conevska, A., Ford, J., Lesnikowski, A., & Harper, S. (2019). Adaptation financing for projects focused on food systems through the UNFCCC. *Climate Policy*, 19(1), 43–58. https://doi.org/10.1080/14693062.2018.1466682.

Constance, D. H., Konefal, J. T., & Hatanaka, M. (2018). *Contested Sustainability Discourses in the Agrifood System*. Routledge.

Conti, C., Zanello, G., & Hall, A. (2021). Why are agri-food systems resistant to new directions of change? A systematic review. *Global Food Security*, 31, 100576. https://doi.org/10.1016/j.gfs.2021.100576.

Convergence. (2021). Blended Finance and Agriculture – Convergence Resources | Convergence. www.convergence.finance/resource/blended-finance-and-agriculture/view.

Conway, G., & Toenniessen, G. (1999). Feeding the world in the twenty-first century. *Nature*, 402(6761), C55.

Cooper, M. (2011). Meeting the demand for evidence-based practice. *Therapy Today*, 22(4), 10–16.

Cornelsen, L., Green, R., Turner, R., et al. (2015). What happens to patterns of food consumption when food prices change? Evidence from a systematic review and meta-analysis of food price elasticities globally. *Health Economics*, 24(12), 1548–1559. https://doi.org/10.1002/hec.3107.

Corvalán Aguilar, C., Reyes, M., Garmendia, M. L., & Uauy Dagach-Imbarack, R. (2013). Structural responses to the obesity and non-communicable diseases epidemic: The Chilean law of food labelling and advertising. *Obesity Reviews*, 14, 79–87. https://doi.org/10.1111/obr.12802.

Crosskey, P. (2016, February 4). A Contested Agroecology – France's Loi d'Avenir | ARC2020. Agricultural and Rural Convention. www.arc2020.eu/a-new-law-a-contested-agroecology-frances-loi-davenir/.

Darnhofer, I. (2015). Socio-technical transitions in farming: Key concepts. In Transition Pathways towards Sustainability in Agriculture: Case Studies from Europe (pp. 17–31). CABI.

de Adelhart Toorop, R., Yates, J., Watkins, M., Bernard, J., & de Groot Ruiz, A. (2021). Methodologies for true cost accounting in the food sector. *Nature Food*, 2(9), 655–663. https://doi.org/10.1038/s43016-021-00364-z.

De Molina, M. G., Petersen, P. F., Peña, F. G., & Caporal, F. R. (2019). Political Agroecology: Advancing the Transition to Sustainable Food Systems. CRC Press.

De Schutter, O. (2014). The specter of productivism and food democracy symposium issue: Safety and sustainability in the era of food systems: Reaching a more integrated approach. *Wisconsin Law Review*, 2014(2), 199–234. https://heinonline.org/HOL/P?h=hein.journals/wlr2014&i=208.

De Schutter, O. (2017). The political economy of food systems reform. *European Review of Agricultural Economics*, 44(4), 705–731. https://doi.org/10.1093/erae/jbx009.

De Schutter, O. (2019). The political economy approach to food systems reform. *IDS Bulletin*, 50(2), 13–26. https://doi.org/10.19088/1968-2019.115.

Den Boer, A. C., Broerse, J. E., & Regeer, B. J. (2021). The need for capacity building to accelerate food system transformation. *Current Opinion in Food Science*, 42, 119–126. https://doi.org/10.1016/j.cofs.2021.05.009.

den Boer, A. C. L., Kok, K. P. W., Gill, M., et al. (2021). Research and innovation as a catalyst for food system transformation. *Trends in Food Science & Technology*, 107, 150–156. https://doi.org/10.1016/j.tifs.2020.09.021.

Denning, G., Kabambe, P., Sanchez, P., et al. (2009). Input subsidies to improve smallholder maize productivity in Malawi: Toward an African green revolution. *PLoS Biology*, 7(1), 002–0010. https://doi.org/10/cr2z93.

Dentoni, D., Waddell, S., & Waddock, S. (2017). Pathways of transformation in global food and agricultural systems: Implications from a large systems change theory perspective. *Current Opinion in Environmental Sustainability*, 29, 8–13. https://doi.org/10.1016/j.cosust.2017.10.003.

Díaz-Bonilla, E. (2023). Financing SDG2 and ending hunger. In J. von Braun, K. Afsana, L. O. Fresco, & M. H. Ali Hassan (Eds.), *Science and Innovations for Food Systems Transformation* (pp. 661–683). Springer.

Diaz-Bonilla, E., McNamara, B., Njuki, J., Swinnen, J., & Vos, R. (2023). The UN Food Systems Summit 2021: Lessons of the Gender and Finance Levers. In Von Braun et al. (Eds.), *Science and Innovations for Food Systems Transformation* (pp. 1–26). Springer. https://doi.org/10.2499/p15738coll2.136685.

Dimas Augusto, D. S., & Rafaela Marinho, D. S. (2024). The police power of the National Health Surveillance Agency – ANVISA. *Archives of Cancer Science and Therapy*, 8(1), 063–076. https://doi.org/10.29328/journal.acst.1001046.

Dixon, J. (2009). From the imperial to the empty calorie: How nutrition relations underpin food regime transitions. *Agriculture and Human Values*, 26(4), 321–333. https://doi.org/10/fsvcv3.

Drummond, E. A. (2013). Global Governance and Food Security Discourses: The FAO and the Via Campesina (Doctoral dissertation, Carleton University).

Dubuisson-Quellier, S., Lamine, C., & Le Velly, R. (2011). Citizenship and consumption: Mobilisation in alternative food systems in France. *Sociologia Ruralis*, 51(3), 304–323. https://doi.org/10.1111/j.1467-9523.2011.00540.x.

Duncan, J., DeClerck, F., Báldi, A., et al. (2022). Democratic directionality for transformative food systems research. *Nature Food*, 3(3), 183–186. https://doi.org/10.1038/s43016-022-00479-x.

Duncan, J., Levkoe, C. Z., & Moragues-Faus, A. (2019). Envisioning new horizons for the political economy of sustainable food systems. *IDS Bulletin*, 50(2), Article 2. https://doi.org/10.19088/1968-2019.117.

DuPuis, E. M., & Goodman, D. (2005). Should we go "home" to eat?: Toward a reflexive politics of localism. *Journal of Rural Studies*, 21(3), 359–371. https://doi.org/10.1016/j.jrurstud.2005.05.011.

Dury, S., Bendjebbar, P., Hainzelin, E., Giordano, T., & Bricas, N. (2019). *Food Systems at Risk: New Trends and Challenges*. CIRAD (Montpellier; France); FAO, CIRAD.

Eakin, H., Connors, J. P., Wharton, C., et al. (2017). Identifying attributes of food system sustainability: Emerging themes and consensus. *Agriculture and Human Values*, 34(3), 757–773. https://doi.org/10.1007/s10460-016-9754-8.

Edwards, F., Sonnino, R., & López Cifuentes, M. (2024). Connecting the dots: Integrating food policies towards food system transformation. *Environmental Science & Policy*, 156, 103735. https://doi.org/10.1016/j.envsci.2024.103735.

El Bilali, H. (2019). The multi-level perspective in research on sustainability transitions in agriculture and food systems: A systematic review. *Agriculture*, 9(4), Article 4. https://doi.org/10.3390/agriculture9040074.

El Bilali, H. (2020). Transition heuristic frameworks in research on agro-food sustainability transitions. *Environment, Development and Sustainability*, 22(3), 1693–1728. https://doi.org/10.1007/s10668-018-0290-0.

Elmqvist, T., Tuvendal, M., Krishnaswamy, J., & Hylander, K. (2013). Chapter 4: Managing Trade-Offs in Ecosystem Services. www.elgaronline.com/edcollchap/edcoll/9781781953686/9781781953686.00010.xml.

Enthoven, L., & Van den Broeck, G. (2021). Local food systems: Reviewing two decades of research. Agricultural Systems, 193, 103226.

ERF. (2008). Defensive R&D and innovation. Highlights note 08. European Risk Forum. http://eriforum.eu/uploads/2/5/7/1/25710097/erf_highlights_8_-_defensive_r_d_and_innovation_-_jul.16.pdf.

ETC Group. (2009). Retooling the planet. Report for Swedish Society for Nature Conservation, December 2009. www.etcgroup.org/sites/www.etcgroup.org/files/publication/pdf_file/Retooling%20the%20Planet%201.2.pdf

ETC Group. (2022). Food Barons 2022 Crisis Profiteering, Digitalization and Shifting Power (Mapping Corporate Power in Food Systems). www.etcgroup.org/sites/www.etcgroup.org/files/files/food-barons-2022-full_sectors-final_16_sept.pdf.

European Commission. Directorate General for Research and Innovation. (2021). Everyone at the table: Co creating knowledge for food systems transformation. Publications Office. https://data.europa.eu/doi/10.2760/21968.

Evans, A., & Miele, M. (2017). Food labelling as a response to political consumption: Effects and contradictions. In M. Keller, B. Halkier, T.-A. Wilska, & M. Truninger (Eds.), *Routledge Handbook on Consumption*. Routledge.

Even, B., Thai, H. T. M., Pham, H. T. M., & Béné, C. (2024). Defining barriers to food systems sustainability: A novel conceptual framework. *Frontiers in Sustainable Food Systems*, 8, 1–17. https://doi.org/10.3389/fsufs.2024.1453999.

Evenson, R. E. (2003). Assessing the impact of the green revolution, 1960 to 2000. *Science*, 300(5620), 758–762. https://doi.org/10/b4vm67.

Fan, S. (2021). Economics in food systems transformation. *Nature Food*, 2(4), 218–219. https://doi.org/10.1038/s43016-021-00266-0.

Fan, S., Headey, D., Rue, C., & Thomas, T. (2021). Food systems for human and planetary health: Economic perspectives and challenges. *Annual Review of Resource Economics*, 13(1), 131–156. https://doi.org/10.1146/annurev-resource-101520-081337.

Fanzo, J., Covic, N., Dobermann, A., et al. (2020). A research vision for food systems in the 2020s: Defying the status quo. *Global Food Security*, 26, 100397. https://doi.org/10.1016/j.gfs.2020.100397.

Fanzo, J., & Davis, C. (2021). Transformations across diets and food systems. In J. Fanzo, & C. Davis (Eds.), *Global Food Systems, Diets, and Nutrition: Linking Science, Economics, and Policy* (pp. 71–84). Springer International. https://doi.org/10.1007/978-3-030-72763-5_6.

Fanzo, J., Haddad, L., Schneider, K. R., et al. (2021). Viewpoint: Rigorous monitoring is necessary to guide food system transformation in the countdown to the 2030 global goals. *Food Policy*, 104, 102163. https://doi.org/10.1016/j.foodpol.2021.102163.

FAO. (2019). A Guide to Resource Mobilization. FAO. www.fao.org/3/i2699e/i2699e00.pdf.

FAO. (2022). Framework for Action on Biodiversity for Food and Agriculture. FAO-FAO Commission on Genetic Resources for Food and Agriculture. https://doi.org/10.4060/cb8338en.

FAO, IFAD, UNICEF, WFP, & WHO. (2021). *The State of Food Security and Nutrition in the World 2021: Transforming Food Systems for Food Security, Improved Nutrition and Affordable Healthy Diets for All*. FAO. www.fao.org/3/cb4474en/cb4474en.pdf.

Feng, S., Zhang, R., & Li, G. (2022). Environmental decentralization, digital finance and green technology innovation. *Structural Change and Economic Dynamics*, 61, 70–83. https://doi.org/10.1016/j.strueco.2022.02.008.

Fernandez-Mena, H., MacDonald, G. K., Pellerin, S., & Nesme, T. (2020). Co-benefits and trade-offs from agro-food system redesign for circularity: A case study with the FAN agent-based model. *Frontiers in Sustainable Food Systems*, 4, 41. https://doi.org/10.3389/fsufs.2020.00041.

Ferraboschi, C., Monroy-Gomez, J., Gavin-Smith, B., et al. (2022). Principles for evidence-based and sustainable food system innovations for healthier diets. *Nutrients*, 14(10), 2003. https://doi.org/10.3390/nu14102003.

FIAN International. (2020). Briefing Note on Multi-Stakeholder. www.fian.org/files/files/Briefing_Note_on_Multi-Stakeholder_Initiatives_Final_e_revised.pdf.

Field, D., & Webb, C. (2022). Momentum is building for a school food program for Canada. *Canadian Food Studies/La Revue Canadienne Des Études Sur l'alimentation*, 9(3), 1–3. https://doi.org/10.15353/cfs-rcea.v9i3.618.

Figeczky, G., Luttikholt, L., Eyhorn, F., et al. (2021). Incentives to change: The experience of the organic sector. In B. Gemmill-Herren, L. E. Baker, & P. A. Daniels (Eds.), *True Cost Accounting for Food*(pp. 1–16). Routledge.

Folke, C., Österblom, H., Jouffray, J.-B., et al. (2019). Transnational corporations and the challenge of biosphere stewardship. *Nature Ecology & Evolution*, 3(10), 1396–1403. https://doi.org/10.1038/s41559-019-0978-z.

Food System Economics Commission. (2024). The Economics of the Food System Transformation. https://foodsystemeconomics.org/wp-content/uploads/FSEC-GlobalPolicyReport-February2024.pdf.

Foran, T., Butler, J. R., Williams, L. J., et al. (2014). Taking complexity in food systems seriously: An interdisciplinary analysis. *World Development*, 61, 85–101. https://doi.org/10.1016/j.worlddev.2014.03.023.

Fox, J. A. (2010). Coalitions and Networks. https://escholarship.org/uc/item/1x05031j.

Fraser, E., Legwegoh, A., Kc, K., et al. (2016). Biotechnology or organic? Extensive or intensive? Global or local? A critical review of potential pathways to resolve the global food crisis. *Trends in Food Science & Technology*, 48, 78–87. https://doi.org/10/ggt37m.

Freeland-Graves, J., & Nitzke, S. (2002). Position of the American Dietetic Association: Total diet approach to communicating food and nutrition information. *Journal of the American Dietetic Association*, 102(1), 100–108. https://doi.org/10.1016/S0002-8223(02)90030-1.

Friedman, N., & Ormiston, J. (2022). Blockchain as a sustainability-oriented innovation?: Opportunities for and resistance to Blockchain technology as a driver of sustainability in global food supply chains. *Technological Forecasting and Social Change*, 175, 121403. https://doi.org/10.1016/j.techfore.2021.121403.

Friedmann, H. (19821982). The political economy of food: The rise and fall of the postwar international food order. *American Journal of Sociology*, 88, S248–S286. https://doi.org/10.1086/649258

Friel, S. (2021). Redressing the corporate cultivation of consumption: Releasing the weapons of the structurally weak. *International Journal of Health Policy and Management*, 10(Special Issue on Political Economy of Food Systems), 784–792. https://doi.org/10.34172/ijhpm.2020.205.

Friel, S., Barosh, L. J., & Lawrence, M. (2014). Towards healthy and sustainable food consumption: An Australian case study. *Public Health Nutrition*, 17(5), 1156–1166. https://doi.org/10.1017/S1368980013001523.

Fulponi, L. (2006). Private voluntary standards in the food system: The perspective of major food retailers in OECD countries. *Food Policy*, 31(1), 1–13. https://doi.org/10.1016/j.foodpol.2005.06.006.

Gabe, K. T., Tramontt, C. R., & Jaime, P. C. (2021). Implementation of food-based dietary guidelines: Conceptual framework and analysis of the Brazilian case. *Public Health Nutrition*, 24(18), 6521–6533. https://doi.org/10.1017/S1368980021003475.

Gaitan-Cremaschi, D., Klerkx, L., Duncan, J., et al. (2019). Characterizing diversity of food systems in view of sustainability transitions: A review. *Agronomy for Sustainable Development*, 39(1), 1. https://doi.org/10.1007/s13593-018-0550-2.

Gale, B. T., & Branch, B. S. (1982). Concentration versus market share: Which determines performance and why does it matter? *The Antitrust Bulletin*, 27(1), 83–105.

Garnett, T. (2013). Food sustainability: Problems, perspectives and solutions. *Proceedings of the Nutrition Society*, 72(1), 29–39. https://doi.org/10/f4jm2v.

Garton, K., Kraak, V., Fanzo, J., et al. (2022). A collective call to strengthen monitoring and evaluation efforts to support healthy and sustainable food systems: "The Accountability Pact." *Public Health Nutrition*, 25(9), 2353–2357. https://doi.org/10.1017/S1368980022001173.

Gawerc, M. I. (2020). Diverse social movement coalitions: Prospects and challenges. *Sociology Compass*, 14(1), e12760. https://doi.org/10.1111/soc4.12760.

Gbejewoh, O., Marais, J., & Erasmus, S. W. (2022). Planetary health and the promises of plant-based meat from a sub-Saharan African perspective: A review. *Scientific African*, 17, 1–12. https://doi.org/10.1016/j.sciaf.2022.e01304.

Geels, F. W. (2002). Technological transitions as evolutionary reconfiguration processes: A multi-level perspective and a case-study. *Research Policy*, 31 (8–9), 1257–1274. https://doi.org/10/dcvxn9.

Geels, F. W. (2005). Processes and patterns in transitions and system innovations: Refining the co-evolutionary multi-level perspective. *Technological Forecasting and Social Change*, 72(6), 681–696. https://doi.org/10/cf4psn.

Geels, F. W. (2011). The multi-level perspective on sustainability transitions: Responses to seven criticisms. *Environmental Innovation and Societal Transitions*, 1(1), 24–40. https://doi.org/10/bz8p6m.

Geels, F. W. (2012). A socio-technical analysis of low-carbon transitions: Introducing the multi-level perspective into transport studies. *Journal of Transport Geography*, 24, 471–482. https://doi.org/10/f4b32f.

Geels, F. W. (2014). Regime resistance against low-carbon transitions: Introducing politics and power into the multi-level perspective. *Theory, Culture & Society*, 31(5), 21–40. https://doi.org/10/gf3t75.

Geels, F. W. (2019). Socio-technical transitions to sustainability: A review of criticisms and elaborations of the multi-level perspective. *Current Opinion in Environmental Sustainability*, 39, 187–201. https://doi.org/10.1016/j.cosust.2019.06.009.

Geels, F. W., & Schot, J. (2007). Typology of sociotechnical transition pathways. *Research Policy*, 36(3), 399–417. https://doi.org/10/dnwt5p.

Gemmill-Herren, B., Baker, L. E., & Daniels, P. A. (2021). *True Cost Accounting for Food: Balancing the Scale*. Taylor & Francis.

Genus, A., & Coles, A.-M. (2008). Rethinking the multi-level perspective of technological transitions. *Research Policy*, 37(9), 1436–1445. https://doi.org/10/bmg57g.

Gies, S. V., Healy, E., & Stephenson, R. (2020). The evidence of effectiveness: Beyond the methodological standards. *Justice Evaluation Journal*, 3(2), 155–177. https://doi.org/10.1080/24751979.2020.1727296.

Gill, M., Den Boer, A. C. L., Kok, K. P. W., et al. (2018). Policy Brief: A Systems Approach to Research and Innovation for Food System Transformation. https://doi.org/10.13140/RG.2.2.19681.97122.

Gillespie, S., Haddad, L., Mannar, V., Menon, P., & Nisbett, N. (2013). The politics of reducing malnutrition: Building commitment and accelerating progress. *The Lancet*, 382(9891), 552–569. https://doi.org/10.1016/S0140-6736(13)60842-9.

Gillespie, S., van den Bold, M., & Hodge, J. (2019). Nutrition and the governance of agri-food systems in South Asia: A systematic review. *Food Policy*, 82, 13–27. https://doi.org/10.1016/j.foodpol.2018.10.013.

Gillespie, S., van den Bold, M., Hodge, J., & Herforth, A. (2015). Leveraging agriculture for nutrition in South Asia and East Africa: Examining the enabling environment through stakeholder perceptions. *Food Security*, 7(3), 463–477. https://doi.org/10.1007/s12571-015-0449-6.

Giner, C., & Brooks, J. (2019). Policies for encouraging healthier food choices (OECD Food, Agriculture and Fisheries Papers 137; OECD Food, Agriculture and Fisheries Papers, Vol. 137). https://doi.org/10.1787/11a42b51-en.

Giuseppe, F. (2015). Global Strategic Framework for Food Security & Nutrition- CFS 2014 Report. https://policycommons.net/artifacts/1619105/

global-strategic-framework-for-food-security-nutrition-cfs-2014-report/ 2309032/.

Global Alliance for Improved Nutrition. (2019). A Review of Business Accountability Mechanisms in Nutrition. Gain. www.gainhealth.org/sites/ default/files/publications/documents/review-of-business-accountability-mechanisms-in-nutrition-report-2019.pdf.

Godek, W. (2021). Food sovereignty policies and the quest to democratize food system governance in Nicaragua. *Agriculture and Human Values*, 38(1), 91–105. https://doi.org/10.1007/s10460-020-10136-3.

Godfray, H. C. J., Beddington, J. R., Crute, I. R., et al. (2010). Food Security: The Challenge of Feeding 9 Billion People. *Science*, 327(5967), 812–818. https://doi.org/10/bhb6zw.

Goldstein, J. E., Neimark, B., Garvey, B., & Phelps, J. (2023). Unlocking "lock-in" and path dependency: A review across disciplines and socio-environmental contexts. *World Development*, 161, 106116. https://doi.org/10.1016/j.worlddev.2022.106116.

Goodman, D., & DuPuis, E. M. (2002). Knowing food and growing food: Beyond the production – Consumption debate in the sociology of agriculture. *Sociologia Ruralis*, 42(1), 5–22. https://doi.org/10/cfg795.

Gottlieb, R., & Fisher, A. (1996). Community food security and environmental justice: Searching for a common discourse. *Agriculture and Human Values*, 13(3), 23–32. https://doi.org/10/cg3b9c.

Gravely, E., & Fraser, E. (2018). Transitions on the shopping floor: Investigating the role of Canadian supermarkets in alternative protein consumption. *Appetite*, 130, 146–156. https://doi.org/10/gfhh56.

Green, R., Cornelsen, L., Dangour, A. D., et al. (2013). The effect of rising food prices on food consumption: Systematic review with meta-regression. *British Medical Journal*, 346, 1–9. https://doi.org/10.1136/bmj.f3703.

Grunert, K. G., Hieke, S., & Wills, J. (2014). Sustainability labels on food products: Consumer motivation, understanding and use. *Food Policy*, 44, 177–189. https://doi.org/10.1016/j.foodpol.2013.12.001.

Grüter, C., & Farina, W. M. (2009). The honeybee waggle dance: Can we follow the steps? *Trends in Ecology & Evolution*, 24(5), 242–247. https://doi.org/10.1016/j.tree.2008.12.007.

Gunderson, R. (2014). Problems with the defetishization thesis: Ethical consumerism, alternative food systems, and commodity fetishism. *Agriculture and Human Values*, 31(1), 109–117. https://doi.org/10.1007/s10460-013-9460-8.

Guo, Z., Bai, L., & Gong, S. (2019). Government regulations and voluntary certifications in food safety in China: A review. *Trends in Food Science & Technology*, 90, 160–165. https://doi.org/10.1016/j.tifs.2019.04.014.

Guthman, J. (2008). Neoliberalism and the making of food politics in California. *Geoforum*, 3(39), 1171–1183. https://doi.org/10.1016/j.geoforum.2006.09.002.

Gyura, G. (2020). Green bonds and green bond funds: The quest for the real impact. *The Journal of Alternative Investments*, 23(1), 71–79.

Habib, M., Singh, S., Bist, Y., et al. (2024). Carbon pricing and the food system: Implications for sustainability and equity. *Trends in Food Science & Technology*, 150, 104577. https://doi.org/10.1016/j.tifs.2024.104577.

Haddad, L., Hawkes, C., Waage, J., et al. (2016). Food Systems and Diets: Facing the Challenges of the 21st Century. Gain, London-UK.

Haddad, L., & Oshaug, A. (1998). How does the human rights perspective help to shape the food and nutrition policy research agenda? *Food Policy*, 23(5), 329–345. https://doi.org/10.1016/S0306-9192(98)00053-0.

Haines, A. (2017). Sugar tax: The winners and losers. *International Tax Review*, 28, 14. https://heinonline.org/HOL/Page?handle=hein.journals/intaxr28&id=152&div=&collection=.

Hainzelin, E., Caron, P., Place, F., et al. (2023). How could science – Policy interfaces boost food system transformation? In J. von Braun, K. Afsana, L. O. Fresco, & M. H. A. Hassan (Eds.), *Science and Innovations for Food Systems Transformation* (pp. 877–891). Springer. https://doi.org/10.1007/978-3-031-15703-5_47.

Harris, J., Anderson, M., Clément, C., & Nisbett, N. (Eds.). (2019). The political economy of food. *IDS Bulletin*, 50(2). IDS. www.academia.edu/49591866/The_Political_Economy_of_Food.

Hashem, K. M., He, F. J., & MacGregor, G. A. (2019). Labelling changes in response to a tax on sugar-sweetened beverages, United Kingdom of Great Britain and Northern Ireland. *Bulletin of the World Health Organization*, 97(12), 818–827. https://doi.org/10.2471/BLT.19.234542.

Hasnain, S., & Chaudhury, A. S. (2021). Financing food system transformation: Insights from global climate projects. *Journal of the British Academy*, 9(s10), 21–42.

Hassanein, N. (2003). Practicing food democracy: A pragmatic politics of transformation. *Journal of Rural Studies*, 19(1), 77–86. https://doi.org/10.1016/S0743-0167(02)00041-4.

Hausmann, R., Klinger, B., & Wagner, R. (2008). Doing growth diagnostics in practice: A'Mindbook'. CID Working Paper Series.

Havemann, T., Negra, C., & Werneck, F. (2022). Blended finance for agriculture: Exploring the constraints and possibilities of combining financial instruments for sustainable transitions. In G. Desa, & X. Jia (Eds.), *Social Innovation and Sustainability Transition* (pp. 347–358). Springer.

Hawkes, C. (2010). 4 – Government and voluntary policies on nutrition labelling: A global overview. In J. Albert (Ed.), *Innovations in Food Labelling* (pp. 37–58). Woodhead. https://doi.org/10.1533/9781845697594.37.

Hebinck, A., Vervoort, J., Hebinck, P., Rutting, L., & Galli, F. (2018). Imagining transformative futures: Participatory foresight for food systems change. *Ecology and Society*, 23(2), 16–35. https://doi.org/10.5751/ES-10054-230216.

Hellin, J., Balié, J., Fisher, E., et al. (2020). Sustainable agriculture for health and prosperity: Stakeholders' roles, legitimacy and modus operandi. *Development in Practice*, 30(7), 965–971. https://doi.org/10.1080/09614524.2020.1798357.

Hendrickson, M. K., Howard, P. H., Miller, E. M., & Constance, D. H. (2020). The food system: Concentration and its impacts. A Special Report to the Family Farm Action Alliance, 17.

Henson, S., & Reardon, T. (2005). Private agri-food standards: Implications for food policy and the agri-food system. *Food Policy*, 30(3), 241–253. https://doi.org/10/cx8nmd.

Herens, M. C., Pittore, K. H., & Oosterveer, P. J. M. (2022). Transforming food systems: Multi-stakeholder platforms driven by consumer concerns and public demands. *Global Food Security-Agriculture Policy Economics and Environment*, 32, 100592. https://doi.org/10.1016/j.gfs.2021.100592.

Hernandez, K., Engler-Stringer, R., Kirk, S., Wittman, H., & McNicholl, S. (2018). The case for a Canadian national school food program. *Canadian Food Studies/La Revue Canadienne Des Études Sur l'alimentation*, 5(3), 208–229. https://doi.org/10.15353/cfs-rcea.v5i3.260.

Herrero, M., Hugas, M., Lele, U., Wirakartakusumah, A., & Torero, M. (2023). A shift to healthy and sustainable consumption patterns. In J. von Braun, K. Afsana, L. O. Fresco, et al. (Eds.), *Science and Innovations for Food Systems Transformation* (pp. 59–85). Springer. https://doi.org/10.1007/978-3-031-15703-5_5.

Herrero, M., Thornton, P. K., Mason-D'Croz, D., et al. (2020). Innovation can accelerate the transition towards a sustainable food system. *Nature Food*, 1(5), 266–272. https://doi.org/10.1038/s43016-020-0074-1.

Herrero, M., Thornton, P. K., Mason-D'Croz, D., et al. (2021). Articulating the effect of food systems innovation on the sustainable development goals. *The Lancet Planetary Health*, 5(1), e50–e62. https://doi.org/10.1016/S2542-5196(20)30277-1.

Herring, R., & Paarlberg, R. (2016). The political economy of biotechnology. *Annual Review of Resource Economics*, 8(1), 397–416. https://doi.org/10/ggt6ds

Hessami, A. R., Faghihi, V., Kim, A., & Ford, D. N. (2020). Evaluating planning strategies for prioritizing projects in sustainability improvement programs. *Construction Management and Economics*, 38(8), 726–738. https://doi.org/10.1080/01446193.2019.1608369.

Higgs, S. (2015). Social norms and their influence on eating behaviours. *Appetite*, 86, 38–44. https://doi.org/10.1016/j.appet.2014.10.021.

Hinrichs, C. C. (2014). Transitions to sustainability: A change in thinking about food systems change? *Agriculture and Human Values*, 31(1), 143–155. https://doi.org/10/f5spqr.

Hinton, L. (2022). Discursive power: Trade over health in CARICOM food labelling policy. *Frontiers in Communication*, 6, 1–15. https://doi.org/10.3389/fcomm.2021.796425.

HLPE. (2017). HLPE Report # 12 – Nutrition and food systems (p. 152). High Level Panel of Experts on Food Security and Nutrition of the Committee on World Food Security.

HLPE. (2019). HLPE Report #14 – Agroecological and other innovative approaches for sustainable agriculture and food systems that enhance food security and nutrition (p. 163). High Level Panel of Experts on Food Security and Nutrition of the Committee on World Food Security.

HLPE. (2020). Food security and nutrition: Building a global narrative towards 2030 (p. 112). High Level Panel of Experts on Food Security and Nutrition of the Committee on World Food Security.

HLPE. (2021). Promoting youth engagement and employment in agriculture and food systems (p. 159). High Level Panel of Experts on Food Security and Nutrition of the Committee on World Food Security.

HLPE. (2022). Data collection and analysis tools for food security and nutrition (p. 154). High Level Panel of Experts on Food Security and Nutrition of the Committee on World Food Security.

Hoek, A. C., Malekpour, S., Raven, R., Court, E., & Byrne, E. (2021). Towards environmentally sustainable food systems: Decision-making factors in sustainable food production and consumption. *Sustainable Production and Consumption*, 26, 610–626. https://doi.org/10.1016/j.spc.2020.12.009.

Hölscher, K., Wittmayer, J. M., & Loorbach, D. (2018). Transition versus transformation: What's the difference? *Environmental Innovation and Societal Transitions*, 27, 1–3. https://doi.org/10.1016/j.eist.2017.10.007.

Holt Giménez, E., & Shattuck, A. (2011). Food crises, food regimes and food movements: Rumblings of reform or tides of transformation? *Journal of Peasant Studies*, 38(1), 109–144. https://doi.org/10.1080/03066150.2010.538578.

Holt-Giménez, E. (2019). Capitalism, food, and social movements: The political economy of food system transformation. *Journal of Agriculture, Food*

Systems, and Community Development, 9(A), Article A. https://doi.org/10.5304/jafscd.2019.091.043.

Holt-Giménez, E., & Altieri, M. A. (2013). Agroecology, food sovereignty, and the new green revolution. *Agroecology and Sustainable Food Systems*, 37(1), 90–102.

Holzer, B. (2006). Political consumerism between individual choice and collective action: Social movements, role mobilization and signalling. *International Journal of Consumer Studies*, 30(5), 405–415. https://doi.org/10.1111/j.1470-6431.2006.00538.x.

Hope Sr, K. R. (2009). Capacity development for good governance in developing countries: Some lessons from the field. *International Journal of Public Administration*, 32(8), 728–740. https://doi.org/10.1080/01900690902908562.

Horbach, J. (Ed.). (2005). *Indicator Systems for Sustainable Innovation*. Physica-Verlag HD. https://doi.org/10.1007/b138695.

Horton, P., Banwart, S. A., Brockington, D., et al. (2017). An agenda for integrated system-wide interdisciplinary agri-food research. *Food Security*, 9(2), 195–210. https://doi.org/10.1007/s12571-017-0648-4.

Hossain, N., & Scott-Villiers, P. (2019). Purchasing and protesting: Power from below in the global food crisis. *IDS Bulletin*, 50(2), Article 2. https://doi.org/10.19088/1968-2019.119.

Hubeau, M., Marchand, F., & Van Huylenbroeck, G. (2017). Sustainability experiments in the agri-food system: Uncovering the factors of new governance and collaboration success. *Sustainability*, 9(6), 1027. https://doi.org/10.3390/su9061027.

Hübel, C., & Schaltegger, S. (2022). Barriers to a sustainability transformation of meat production practices – An industry actor perspective. *Sustainable Production and Consumption*, 29, 128–140. https://doi.org/10.1016/j.spc.2021.10.004.

Hunter, D., Özkan, I., Moura de Oliveira Beltrame, D., et al. (2016). Enabled or disabled: Is the environment right for using biodiversity to improve nutrition? *Frontiers in Nutrition*, 3(14), 1–5. https://doi.org/10.3389/fnut.2016.00014.

Hutter, L., & Lawrence, H. (2021). The discourse of technological innovation: A new domain for accountability. *Proceedings of the 39th ACM International Conference on Design of Communication*, 151–156. https://doi.org/10.1145/3472714.3473635.

Imran, M., & Imran, A. (Eds.). (2020). *Malnutrition*. BoD – Books on Demand.

Ingram, J. (2011). A food systems approach to researching food security and its interactions with global environmental change. *Food Security*, 3(4), 417–431. https://doi.org/10/bgcvzg.

Ingram, J. (2015). Framing niche-regime linkage as adaptation: An analysis of learning and innovation networks for sustainable agriculture across Europe. *Journal of Rural Studies*, 40, 59–75. https://doi.org/10.1016/j.jrurstud.2015.06.003.

Ip, S., Chung, M., Raman, G., et al. (2007). Breastfeeding and maternal and infant health outcomes in developed countries. *Evidence Report/Technology Assessment*, 153, 1–186.

IPBES. (2017). Trade-Off. www.ipbes.net/glossary/trade.

IPES-Food. (2016). From uniformity to diversity: A paradigm shift from industrial agriculture to diversified agroecological systems. International Panel of Experts on Sustainable Food systems. www.ipes-food.org/_img/upload/files/UniformityToDiversity_FULL.pdf.

IPES-Food. (2017). Too big to feed: Exploring the impacts of mega-mergers, concentration, concentration of power in the agri-food sector. IPES-Food. www.ipes-food.org/_img/upload/files/Concentration_FullReport.pdf.

IPES-Food. (2023). Who's Tipping the Scales? The growing influence of corporations on the governance of food systems, and how to counter it. IPES. www.ipes-food.org/_img/upload/files/tippingthescales.pdf.

IPES-Food & ETC Group. (2021). Long Food Movement: Transforming Food Systems by 2045. IPES-Food. www.ipes-food.org/_img/upload/files/LongFoodMovementEN.pdf.

Jacobsen, E., & Dulsrud, A. (2007). Will consumers save the world? The framing of political consumerism. *Journal of Agricultural and Environmental Ethics*, 20(5), 469–482. https://doi.org/10.1007/s10806-007-9043-z.

Jagustovic, R., Papachristos, G., Zougmore, R. B., et al. (2021). Better before worse trajectories in food systems? An investigation of synergies and trade-offs through climate-smart agriculture and system dynamics. *Agricultural Systems*, 190, 103131. https://doi.org/10.1016/j.agsy.2021.103131.

Jahiel, R. I., & Babor, T. F. (2007). Industrial epidemics, public health advocacy and the alcohol industry: Lessons from other fields [Editorial]. *Addiction*, 102(9), 1335–1339. https://doi.org/10.1111/j.1360-0443.2007.01900.x

Jayne, T. s., & Rashid, S. (2013). Input subsidy programs in sub-Saharan Africa: A synthesis of recent evidence. *Agricultural Economics*, 44(6), 547–562. https://doi.org/10.1111/agec.12073.

Jensen, N. H., & Lieberoth, A. (2019). We will eat disgusting foods together – Evidence of the normative basis of western entomophagy-disgust from an insect tasting. *Food Quality and Preference*, 72, 109–115. https://doi.org/10.1016/j.foodqual.2018.08.012.

Jia, X. (2021). Agro-food innovation and sustainability transition: A conceptual synthesis. *Sustainability*, 13(12), 6897. https://doi.org/10.3390/su13126897.

Jirström, M. (2005). The state and green revolutions in East Asia. In G. Djurfeldt, H. Holmén, M. Jirström, & R. Larsson (Eds.), *The African Food Crisis: Lessons from the Asian Green Revolution* (pp. 25–42). CABI.

Juri, S., Baraibar, M., Clark, L. B., et al. (2022). Food systems transformations in South America: Insights from a transdisciplinary process rooted in Uruguay. *Frontiers in Sustainable Food Systems*, 6, 887034. https://doi.org/10.3389/fsufs.2022.887034.

Kampman, H., Zongrone, A., Rawat, R., & Becquey, E. (2017). How Senegal created an enabling environment for nutrition: A story of change. *Global Food Security*, 13, 57–65. https://doi.org/10.1016/j.gfs.2017.02.005.

Kang, H., Roggio, A. M., & Luna-Reyes, L. F. (2022). Governance of local food systems: Current research and future directions. *Journal of Cleaner Production*, 338, 130626. https://doi.org/10.1016/j.jclepro.2022.130626.

Kansanga, M., Andersen, P., Kpienbaareh, D., et al. (2018). Traditional agriculture in transition: Examining the impacts of agricultural modernization on smallholder farming in Ghana under the new Green Revolution. *International Journal of Sustainable Development & World Ecology*, 26(1), 11–24. https://doi.org/10/ggt34c.

Kanter, D. R., Schwoob, M.-H., Baethgen, W. E., et al. (2016). Translating the sustainable development goals into action: A participatory backcasting approach for developing national agricultural transformation pathways. *Global Food Security*, 10, 71–79. https://doi.org/10.1016/j.gfs.2016.08.002.

Kato, T., & Greeley, M. (2016). Agricultural input subsidies in sub-Saharan Africa. *IDS Bulletin*, 47(2), 33–48. https://doi.org/10.19088/1968-2016.130.

Keeley, J., & Scoones, I. (2000). Knowledge, power and politics: The environmental policy-making process in Ethiopia. *The Journal of Modern African Studies*, 38(1), 89–120. https://doi.org/10.1017/S0022278X99003262.

Keller, M., Halkier, B., Wilska, T.-A., & Truninger, M. (2017). *Routledge Handbook on Consumption*. Taylor & Francis.

Kemp, R. (2010). Sustainable technologies do not exist! EKONOMIAZ. *Revista Vasca de Economía*, 75(4), 22–39. https://ideas.repec.org//a/ekz/ekonoz/2010403.html.

Kemper, J. A., & Ballantine, P. W. (2017). Socio-technical transitions and institutional change: Addressing obesity through macro-social marketing. *Journal of Macromarketing*, 37(4), 381–392. https://doi.org/10.1177/0276146717715746.

Kennedy, E., Webb, P., Block, S., et al. (2021). Transforming food systems: The missing pieces needed to make them work. *Current Developments in Nutrition*, 5(1), 5001007. https://doi.org/10.1093/cdn/nzaa177.

Kerali, H. R., & Mannisto, V. (1999). Prioritization methods for strategic planning and road work programming in a new highway development and management tool. *Transportation Research Record*, 1655(1), 49–54. https://doi.org/10.3141/1655-08.

Kerr, R. B., Madsen, S., Stüber, M., et al. (2021). Can agroecology improve food security and nutrition? A review. Global Food Security, 29, 100540.

Khadse, A., Rosset, P. M., Morales, H., & Ferguson, B. G. (2018). Taking agroecology to scale: The zero budget natural farming peasant movement in Karnataka, India. *The Journal of Peasant Studies*, 45(1), 192–219. https://doi.org/10.1080/03066150.2016.1276450.

Khan, N., Ray, R. L., Kassem, H. S., et al. (2021). Potential role of technology innovation in transformation of sustainable food systems: A review. *Agriculture*, 11(10), 984. https://doi.org/10.3390/agriculture11100984.

Kiesel, L. (2010). A comparative rhetorical analysis of US and UK newspaper coverage of the correlation between livestock production and climate change. Environmental Communication as a Nexus. *Proceedings of the 10th Biennial Conference on Communication and the Environment*, 247–255.

Kimenju, S. C., De Groote, H., Karugia, J., Mbogoh, S., & Poland, D. (2005). Consumer awareness and attitudes toward GM foods in Kenya. *African Journal of Biotechnology*, 4(10), 1066–1075.

Kirchherr, J., Piscicelli, L., Bour, R., et al. (2018). Barriers to the circular economy: Evidence from the European Union (EU). *Ecological Economics*, 150, 264–272. https://doi.org/10.1016/j.ecolecon.2018.04.028.

Kitaoka, K. (2018). The national school meal program in Brazil: A literature review. *The Japanese Journal of Nutrition and Dietetics*, 76(Supplement), S115–S125. https://doi.org/10.5264/eiyogakuzashi.76.S115.

Klassen, S., Medland, L., Nicol, P., & Pitt, H. (2023). Pathways for advancing good work in food systems: Reflecting on the international good work for good food forum. *Journal of Agriculture, Food Systems, and Community Development*, 12(2), 249–265. https://doi.org/10.5304/jafscd.2023.122.004.

Klerkx, L., & Begemann, S. (2020). Supporting food systems transformation: The what, why, who, where and how of mission-oriented agricultural innovation systems. *Agricultural Systems*, 184, 102901. https://doi.org/10.1016/j.agsy.2020.102901.

Knight, F., Bourassa, M. W., Ferguson, E., et al. (2022). Nutrition modeling tools: A qualitative study of influence on policy decision making and determining factors. *Annals of the New York Academy of Sciences*, 1513(1), 170–191. https://doi.org/10.1111/nyas.14778.

Knößlsdorfer, I., Sellare, J., & Qaim, M. (2021). Effects of fairtrade on farm household food security and living standards: Insights from Côte d'Ivoire. *Global Food Security*, 29, 100535. https://doi.org/10.1016/j.gfs.2021.100535.

Kraak, V. I., Swinburn, B., Lawrence, M., & Harrison, P. (2014). An accountability framework to promote healthy food environments. *Public Health Nutrition*, 17(11), 2467–2483. https://doi.org/10.1017/S1368980014000093.

Krasny, J. (2012). Every parent should know the scandalous history of infant formula. *Business Insider*, 25, 3319–3354.

Kuchiki, A. (2004). Prioritization of Policies: A Prototype Model of a Flowchart Method. Institute of Developing Economies, Japan External Trade Organization(JETRO), IDE Discussion Papers.

Kugelberg, S., Bartolini, F., Kanter, D. R., et al. (2021). Implications of a food system approach for policy agenda-setting design. *Global Food Security-Agriculture Policy Economics and Environment*, 28, 100451. https://doi.org/10.1016/j.gfs.2020.100451.

Kuiper, M. H., Zurek, M., Havlik, P., et al. (2017). Deliverable No. 1.4: A Modelling Strategy for Quantifying the Sustainability of Food and Nutrition Security in the EU. SUSFANS.

Kushitor, S. B., Drimie, S., Davids, R., et al. (2022). The complex challenge of governing food systems: The case of South African food policy. *Food Security*, 14(4), 883–896. https://doi.org/10.1007/s12571-022-01258-z.

Lachman, D. A. (2013). A survey and review of approaches to study transitions. *Energy Policy*, 58, 269–276. https://doi.org/10.1016/j.enpol.2013.03.013.

Lam, D. P. M., Jiménez-Aceituno, A., Guerrero Lara, L., et al. (2022). Amplifying actions for food system transformation: Insights from the Stockholm region. *Sustainability Science*, 17(6), 2379–2395. https://doi.org/10.1007/s11625-022-01154-7.

Lartey, A., Meerman, J., & Wijesinha-Bettoni, R. (2018). Why food system transformation is essential and how nutrition scientists can contribute. *Annals of Nutrition and Metabolism*, 72(3), 193–201. https://doi.org/10.1159/000487605.

Lawal, G. (2007). Corruption and development in Africa: Challenges for political and economic change. *Humanity and Social Sciences Journal*, 2(1), 1–7.

Lawhon, M., & Murphy, J. T. (2012). Socio-technical regimes and sustainability transitions: Insights from political ecology. *Progress in Human Geography*, 36(3), 354–378. https://doi.org/10/cxngxf.

Lea, E., & Worsley, A. (2001). Influences on meat consumption in Australia. *Appetite*, 36(2), 127–136. https://doi.org/10.1006/appe.2000.0386.

Leach, M., Nisbett, N., Cabral, L., et al. (2020). Food politics and development. *World Development*, 134, 105024. https://doi.org/10.1016/j.worlddev.2020.105024.

Leeuwis, C., Boogaard, B. K., & Atta-Krah, K. (2021). How food systems change (or not): Governance implications for system transformation processes. *Food Security*, 13(4), 761–780. https://doi.org/10.1007/s12571-021-01178-4.

Legwegoh, A. F., & Fraser, E. D. G. (2015). Food crisis or chronic poverty: Metanarratives of food insecurity in sub-Saharan Africa. *Journal of Hunger & Environmental Nutrition*, 10(3), 313–342. https://doi.org/10/ggt3tc.

Lentz, E. C. (2021). Food and agriculture systems foresight study: Implications for gender, poverty, and nutrition. *Q Open*, 1(1), qoaa003. https://doi.org/10.1093/qopen/qoaa003.

Levkoe, C. Z., & Sheedy, A. (2018). A people-centred approach to food policy making: Lessons from Canada's people's food policy project. *Journal of Hunger & Environmental Nutrition*, 14(3), 3183–338. www.academia.edu/35441272/A_people-centred_approach_to_food_policy_making_Lessons_from_Canadas_Peoples_Food_Policy_project.

Limketka, B., Guarnaschelli, S., & Millan, A. (2020). Financing the Transformation of Food Systems under a Changing Climate. CCAFS. https://cgspace.cgiar.org/bitstream/handle/10568/101132/CCAFS%20KOIS%20Financing%20the%20Transformation%20of%20Food%20Systems%20Under%20a%20Changing%20Climate.pdf?sequence=1&isAllowed=y.

Lipper, L., Cavatassi, R., Symons, R., Gordes, A., & Page, O. (2021). Financing adaptation for resilient livelihoods under food system transformation: The role of multilateral development banks. *Food Security*, 13, 1–16.

Lizie, A. (2012). Food and communication. In K. Albala (Ed.), *Routledge International Handbook of Food Studies* (pp. 27–38). () Routledge.

Lockie, S. (2002). "The invisible mouth": Mobilizing "the consumer" in food production – Consumption networks. *Sociologia Ruralis*, 42(4), 278–294. https://doi.org/10.1111/1467-9523.00217.

Macdiarmid, J. I., Douglas, F., & Campbell, J. (2016). Eating like there's no tomorrow: Public awareness of the environmental impact of food and reluctance to eat less meat as part of a sustainable diet. *Appetite*, 96, 487–493. https://doi.org/10.1016/j.appet.2015.10.011.

Macdonald, K. (2007). Globalising justice within coffee supply chains? Fair trade, Starbucks and the transformation of supply chain governance. *Third World Quarterly*, 28(4), 793–812. https://doi.org/10.1080/01436590701336663.

MacRae, R., & Abergel, E. (2012). *Health and Sustainability in the Canadian Food System: Advocacy and Opportunity for Civil Society*. UBC Press.

Mahumud, R. A., Uprety, S., Wali, N., Renzaho, A. M. N., & Chitekwe, S. (2022). The effectiveness of interventions on nutrition social behaviour change communication in improving child nutritional status within the first 1000 days: Evidence from a systematic review and meta-analysis. *Maternal & Child Nutrition*, 18(1), e13286. https://doi.org/10.1111/mcn.13286.

Maltais, A., & Nykvist, B. (2020). Understanding the role of green bonds in advancing sustainability. *Journal of Sustainable Finance & Investment*, 0(0), 1–20. https://doi.org/10.1080/20430795.2020.1724864.

Manorat, R., Becker, L., & Flory, A. (2019). Global data visualization tools to empower decision-making in nutrition. *Sight and Life*, 33(1), 108–114.

Marsden, T., Hebinck, P., & Mathijs, E. (2018). Re-building food systems: Embedding assemblages, infrastructures and reflexive governance for food systems transformations in Europe. *Food Security*, 10(6), 1301–1309. https://doi.org/10.1007/s12571-018-0870-8.

Marshall, Q., Bellows, A. L., McLaren, R., Jones, A. D., & Fanzo, J. (2021). You say you want a data revolution? Taking on food systems accountability. *Agriculture*, 11(5), Article 5. https://doi.org/10.3390/agriculture11050422.

Martinez, S. (2010). Local Food Systems; Concepts, Impacts, and Issues. Diane Publishing.

Marzeda-Mlynarska, K. (2011). The application of multi-level governance model outside the EU-context: The case of food security. *European Diversity and Autonomy Papers-EDAP*, 2011(1), 1–11.

Masters, W. A., Rosettie, K., Kranz, S., et al. (2018). Priority interventions to improve maternal and child diets in sub-Saharan Africa and South Asia. *Maternal and Child Nutrition*, 14(2), 1–11. https://doi.org/10/ggfp9x.

Matthews, N. E., Stamford, L., & Shapira, P. (2019). Aligning sustainability assessment with responsible research and innovation: Towards a framework for Constructive Sustainability Assessment. *Sustainable Production and Consumption*, 20, 58–73. https://doi.org/10.1016/j.spc.2019.05.002.

Mattioni, D., Milbourne, P., & Sonnino, R. (2022). Destabilizing the food regime "from within": Tools and strategies used by urban food policy actors. *Environmental Innovation and Societal Transitions*, 44, 48–59. https://doi.org/10.1016/j.eist.2022.05.007.

Mausch, K., Hall, A., & Hambloch, C. (2020). Colliding paradigms and trade-offs: Agri-food systems and value chain interventions. *Global Food Security*, 26, 100439. https://doi.org/10.1016/j.gfs.2020.100439.

Maye, D. (2013). Moving alternative food networks beyond the niche. *The International Journal of Sociology of Agriculture and Food*, 20(3), 383–389.

Mazzucato, M. (2016). From market fixing to market-creating: A new framework for innovation policy. *Industry and Innovation*, 23(2), 140–156. https://doi.org/10.1080/13662716.2016.1146124.

McDermid, S. S., Hayek, M., Jamieson, D. W., Hale, G., & Kanter, D. (2023). Research needs for a food system transition. *Climatic Change*, 176(4), 41. https://doi.org/10.1007/s10584-023-03507-2.

McKeon, N. (2014). *Food Security Governance: Empowering Communities, Regulating Corporations*. Routledge.

McMichael, P. (2021). Shock and awe in the UNFSS. *Development*, 64(3), 162–171. https://doi.org/10.1057/s41301-021-00304-1.

McNeill, D. (2019). Reflections on IPES-food: Can power analysis change the world? *IDS Bulletin*, 50(2), 27–36. https://doi.org/10.19088/1968-2019.116.

Michalke, A., Köhler, S., Messmann, L., et al. (2023). True cost accounting of organic and conventional food production. *Journal of Cleaner Production*, 408, 137134. https://doi.org/10.1016/j.jclepro.2023.137134.

Milat, A. J., & Li, B. (2017). Narrative review of frameworks for translating research evidence into policy and practice. *Public Health Research & Practice*, 27(1), 1–13., https://doi.org/10.17061/phrp2711704.

Miles, A., DeLonge, M. S., & Carlisle, L. (2017a). Triggering a positive research and policy feedback cycle to support a transition to agroecology and sustainable food systems. *Agroecology and Sustainable Food Systems*, 41(7), 855–879. https://doi.org/10.1080/21683565.2017.1331179.

Miles, A., DeLonge, M. S., & Carlisle, L. (2017b). Triggering a positive research and policy feedback cycle to support a transition to agroecology and sustainable food systems. *Agroecology and Sustainable Food Systems*, 41(7), 855–879. https://doi.org/10.1080/21683565.2017.1331179.

Millan, A., Limketkai, B., & Guarnaschelli, S. (2019). Financing the transformation of food systems under a changing climate. CCAFS Report. Wageningen, The Netherlands: CGIAR Research Program on Climate Change, Agriculture and Food Security (CCAFS). https://hdl.handle.net/10568/101132

Miller, B. (2021). Is technology value-neutral? *Science, Technology, & Human Values*, 46(1), 53–80. https://doi.org/10.1177/0162243919900965.

Montenegro de Wit, M., & Iles, A. (2021). Woke science and the 4th industrial revolution: Inside the making of UNFSS knowledge. *Development*, 64(3), 199–211. https://doi.org/10.1057/s41301-021-00314-z.

Moodie, R., Bennett, E., Kwong, E. J. L., et al. (2021). Ultra-processed profits: The political economy of countering the global spread of ultra-processed foods – A synthesis review on the market and political practices of transnational food corporations and strategic public health responses. *International Journal of Health Policy and Management*, 10(Special Issue on Political Economy of Food Systems), 968–982. https://doi.org/10.34172/ijhpm.2021.45.

Morgan, K., & Sonnino, R. (2013). *The School Food Revolution: Public Food and the Challenge of Sustainable Development*. Routledge.

Morkel, C., & Ramasobama, M. (2017). Measuring the effect of evaluation capacity building initiatives in Africa: A review. *African Evaluation Journal*, 5(1), 1–12. https://doi.org/10.4102/aej.v5i1.187.

Muller, M. (1975). *The baby killer; a War on Want investigation into the promotion and sale of powdered baby milks in the third world-2* (2nd edition). AGRIS, FAO.

Mvondo, S. A. (2009). State failure and governance in vulnerable states: An assessment of forest law compliance and enforcement in Cameroon. *Africa Today*, 55(3), 85–102. https://doi.org/10.2979/AFT.2009.55.3.84.

Neff, R. A., Chan, I. L., & Smith, K. C. (2009). Yesterday's dinner, tomorrow's weather, today's news? US newspaper coverage of food system contributions to climate change. *Public Health Nutrition*, 12(7), 1006–1014. https://doi.org/10.1017/S1368980008003480.

Negra, C., Remans, R., Attwood, S., Jones, S., Werneck, F., & Smith, A. (2020). Sustainable agri-food investments require multi-sector co-development of decision tools. *Ecological Indicators*, 110, 105851.

Nelson, V., & Tallontire, A. (2014). Battlefields of ideas: Changing narratives and power dynamics in private standards in global agricultural value chains. *Agriculture and Human Values*, 31(3), 481–497. https://doi.org/10.1007/s10460-014-9512-8.

Newell, P. (2008). Civil society, corporate accountability and the politics of climate change. *Global Environmental Politics*, 8(3), 122–153. https://doi.org/10.1162/glep.2008.8.3.122.

Ngqangashe, Y., & Friel, S. (2022). Regulatory governance pathways to improve the efficacy of Australian food policies. *Australian and New Zealand Journal of Public Health*, 46(5), 710–715. https://doi.org/10.1111/1753-6405.13284.

Nidumolu, R., Prahalad, C. K., & Rangaswami, M. R. (2009, September 1). Why sustainability is now the key driver of innovation. *Harvard Business Review*, 87(9), 56–64. https://hbr.org/2009/09/why-sustainability-is-now-the-key-driver-of-innovation.

Niederle, P., Petersen, P., Coudel, E., et al. (2023). Ruptures in the agroecological transitions: Institutional change and policy dismantling in Brazil. *The Journal of Peasant Studies*, 50(3), 931–953. https://doi.org/10.1080/03066150.2022.2055468.

Nisbett, N., Gillespie, S., Haddad, L., & Harris, J. (2014). Why worry about the politics of childhood undernutrition? *World Development*, 64, 420–433. https://doi.org/10.1016/j.worlddev.2014.06.018.

Noack, A.-L., & Pouw, N. R. M. (2015). A blind spot in food and nutrition security: Where culture and social change shape the local food plate. *Agriculture and Human Values*, 32(2), 169–182. https://doi.org/10.1007/s10460-014-9538-y.

Nyantakyi-Frimpong, H., & Bezner Kerr, R. (2015). A political ecology of high-input agriculture in Northern Ghana. *African Geographical Review*, 34(1), 13–35. https://doi.org/10/ggt375.

Nyborg, K., Anderies, J. M., Dannenberg, A., et al. (2016). Social norms as solutions. *Science*, 354(6308), 42–43. https://doi.org/10.1126/science.aaf8317.

O'Brien, E., & Macoun, A. (2022). Responsible citizens, political consumers and the state. *Acta Politica*, 57(2), 377–395. https://doi.org/10.1057/s41269-021-00194-8.

OECD. (2010). *Multi-Level Governance: A Conceptual Framework* (pp. 171–178). OECD. https://doi.org/10.1787/9789264091375-11-en.

OECD. (2015). Better Policies for Development 2015: Policy Coherence and Green Growth. OECD. https://doi.org/10.1787/9789264236813-en.

OECD. (2016). Better Policies for Sustainable Development 2016: A New Framework for Policy Coherence. OECD. https://doi.org/10.1787/9789264256996-en.

OECD & FAO. (2021). Meat. In OECD & Food and Agriculture Organization of the United Nations, OECD-FAO *Agricultural Outlook* 2021–2030. OECD. https://doi.org/10.1787/cf68bf79-en.

Elechi, J. Okoro Godwin, Nwiyi, I. U., & Adamu, C. S. (2022). Global food system transformation for resilience. In A. I. Ribeiro-Barros, D. S. Tevera, L. F. Goulao, & L. D. Tivana (Eds.), *Sustainable Development* (Vol. 1, pp. 1–29). IntechOpen. www.intechopen.com/chapters/81235.

Oliver, T. H., Boyd, E., Balcombe, K., et al. (2018). Overcoming undesirable resilience in the global food system. *Global Sustainability*, 1, e9. https://doi.org/10.1017/sus.2018.9.

Olsson, P., Galaz, V., & Boonstra, W. J. (2014). Sustainability transformations: A resilience perspective. *Ecology and Society*, 19(4), 1–13. https://doi.org/10.5751/ES-06799-190401.

Pamuk, H., & Rijn, F. V. (2018). The impact of innovation platform diversity in agricultural network formation and technology adoption: Evidence from sub-Saharan Africa. *The Journal of Development Studies*, 55(6), 1240–1252., www.tandfonline.com/doi/abs/10.1080/00220388.2018.1453606.

Park, H., & Kim, J. D. (2020). Transition towards green banking: Role of financial regulators and financial institutions. *Asian Journal of Sustainability and Social Responsibility*, 5(1), 1–25. https://doi.org/10.1186/s41180-020-00034-3.

Parsons, K., & Barling, D. (2021). Food Systems Transformation: What's in the Policy Toolbox? http://uhra.herts.ac.uk/handle/2299/25340.

Parsons, K., & Hawkes, C. (2019). Policy Coherence in Food Systems. https://researchprofiles.herts.ac.uk/en/publications/policy-coherence-in-food-systems.

Patel, R. (2013). The Long Green Revolution. *Journal of Peasant Studies*, 40(1), 1–63. https://doi.org/10/gf5257.

Peekhaus, W. (2010). Monsanto Discovers New Social Media. *International Journal of Communication*, 4, 955–976.

Pelling, M. (2010). *Adaptation to Climate Change: From Resilience to Transformation*. Routledge.

Pelling, M., O'Brien, K., & Matyas, D. (2015). Adaptation and transformation. *Climatic Change*, 133(1), 113–127. https://doi.org/10/f7v2gk.

Pereira, L., & Drimie, S. (2016). Governance arrangements for the future food system: Addressing complexity in South Africa. *Environment: Science and Policy for Sustainable Development*, 58(4), 18–31. https://doi.org/10.1080/00139157.2016.1186438.

Pereira, L. M., Drimie, S., Maciejewski, K., Tonissen, P. B., & Biggs, R. (Oonsie). (2020). Food system transformation: Integrating a political – Economy and social – Ecological approach to regime shifts. *International Journal of Environmental Research and Public Health*, 17(4), 1313. https://doi.org/10.3390/ijerph17041313.

Pignatti, E., Carli, G., & Canavari, M. (2015). What really matters? A qualitative analysis on the adoption of innovations in agriculture. *Journal of Agricultural Informatics*, 6(4), Article 4. https://doi.org/10.17700/jai.2015.6.4.212.

Pingali, P. (2007). Westernization of Asian diets and the transformation of food systems: Implications for research and policy. *Food Policy*, 32(3), 281–298. https://doi.org/10.1016/j.foodpol.2006.08.001.

Pitt, H., & Jones, M. (2016). Scaling up and out as a pathway for food system transitions. *Sustainability*, 8(10), 1–16.

Pohjolainen, P., Tapio, P., Vinnari, M., Jokinen, P., & Räsänen, P. (2016). Consumer consciousness on meat and the environment – Exploring differences. *Appetite*, 11(101), 37–45. https://doi.org/10.1016/j.appet.2016.02.012.

Politico. (2022, March 10). Addressing harmful subsidies globally will help solve the climate and biodiversity crises. *POLITICO*. www.politico.eu/sponsored-content/climate-change-and-biodiversity-loss-are-the-twin-crises-of-our-era-reforming-agricultural-fishery-and-forestry-subsidies-could-help-solve-both/.

Popkin, B. M., & Reardon, T. (2018). Obesity and the food system transformation in Latin America. *Obesity Reviews*, 19(8), 1028–1064. https://doi.org/10.1111/obr.12694.

Poponi, S., Arcese, G., Pacchera, F., & Martucci, O. (2022). Evaluating the transition to the circular economy in the agri-food sector: Selection of indicators. *Resources, Conservation and Recycling*, 176, 105916. https://doi.org/10.1016/j.resconrec.2021.105916.

Post, L., Schmitz, A., Issa, T., & Oehmke, J. (2021). Enabling the environment for private sector investment: Impact on food security and poverty. *Journal of Agricultural & Food Industrial Organization*, 19(1), 25–37. https://doi.org/10.1515/jafio-2021-0013.

Potter, C., & Brough, R. (2004). Systemic capacity building: A hierarchy of needs. *Health Policy and Planning*, 19(5), 336–345. https://doi.org/10.1093/heapol/czh038.

Prost, S. (2019). Food democracy for all? Developing a food hub in the context of socio-economic deprivation. *Politics and Governance*, 7(4), 142–153. https://doi.org/10.17645/pag.v7i4.2057.

Pudjiastuti, S. R. (2021). Global issues of environmental law enforcement impacts on sustainable development. *Jhss (Journal of Humanities and Social Studies)*, 5(1), 56–62. https://doi.org/10.33751/jhss.v5i1.3226.

Qiao, Y., Martin, F., He, X., Zhen, H., & Pan, X. (2019). The changing role of local government in organic agriculture development in Wanzai County, China. *Canadian Journal of Development Studies / Revue Canadienne d'études Du Développement*, 40(1), 64–77. https://doi.org/10.1080/02255189.2019.1520693.

Quested, T. E., Marsh, E., Stunell, D., & Parry, A. D. (2013). Spaghetti soup: The complex world of food waste behaviours. *Resources, Conservation and Recycling*, 79, 43–51. https://doi.org/10.1016/j.resconrec.2013.04.011.

Raja, S., Raj, S., & Roberts, B. (2017). The US experience in planning for community food systems: An era of advocacy, awareness, and (some) learning. In I. Knezevic, A. Blay-Palmer, C. Z. Levkoe, P. Mount, & E. Nelson (Eds.), *Nourishing Communities: From Fractured Food Systems to Transformative Pathways* (pp. 59–74). Springer International. https://doi.org/10.1007/978-3-319-57000-6_4.

Reisch, L., Eberle, U., & Lorek, S. (2013). Sustainable food consumption: An overview of contemporary issues and policies. *Sustainability: Science, Practice and Policy*, 9(2), 7–25. https://doi.org/10.1080/15487733.2013.11908111.

Remans, R., Zornetzer, H., Mason-D'Croz, D., et al. (2024). Backcasting supports cross-sectoral collaboration and social-technical innovation bundling: Case studies in agri-food systems. *Frontiers in Sustainable Food Systems*, 8, 1–12. https://doi.org/10.3389/fsufs.2024.1378883.

Renick, D. (2020). The political economy of agricultural policy in Africa: Implications for agrifood system transformation (Chapter 14). Annual Trends and Outlook Report. International Food Policy Research Institute. https://doi.org/10.2499/9780896293946_14.

Renting, H., & Wiskerke, H. (2010). New emerging roles for public institutions and civil society in the promotion of sustainable local agro-food systems. In I. Darnhofer, & M. Grotzer (Eds.), *Building Sustainable Rural Futures: The*

Added Value of Systems Approaches in Times of Change and Uncertainty (pp. 1902–1912). BOKU - University of Natural Resources and Applied Life Sciences.

Richardson, L., & Fernqvist, F. (2022). Transforming the food system through sustainable gastronomy – How chefs engage with food democracy. *Journal of Hunger & Environmental Nutrition*, 19(2), 260–276. https://doi.org/10.1080/19320248.2022.2059428.

Ridolfi, R., Dernini, S., Morrison, J., Mathiesen, Á. M., & Capone, R. (2020). Changing route: Common action on food systems transformation in the Mediterranean. *New Medit: Mediterranean Journal of Economics, Agriculture and Environment/Revue Méditerranéenne d'Economie Agriculture et Environment*, 19(3), 119–128. https://doi.org/10.30682/nm2003h2

Rip, A., & Kemp, R. (1998). Technological change. *Human Choice and Climate Change*, 2(2), 327–399.

Roache, S. A., & Gostin, L. O. (2017). The untapped power of soda taxes: Incentivizing consumers, generating revenue, and altering corporate behavior. *International Journal of Health Policy and Management*, 6(9), 489. https://doi.org/10.15171/ijhpm.2017.69.

Rogers, E. M. (1983). *Diffusion of Innovations* (3rd ed). Free Press [u.a.].

Roggio, A. M., & Evans, J. R. (2022). Will participatory guarantee systems happen here? The case for innovative food systems governance in the developed world. *Sustainability*, 14(3), 1720. https://doi.org/10.3390/su14031720.

Rondinelli, D. A. (2017). Decentralization and development. In A. Shafiqul Huque, & H. Zafarullah (Eds.), *International Development Governance* (pp. 391–404). Routledge.

Rose, F. (2000). *Coalitions across the Class Divide: Lessons from the Labor, Peace, and Environmental Movements*. Cornell University Press.

Rose, N. (2015). *Fair Food: Stories from a Movement Changing the World*. University of Queensland Press.

Rossi, L., Ferrari, M., Martone, D., Benvenuti, L., & De Santis, A. (2021). The promotions of sustainable lunch meals in school feeding programs: The case of Italy. *Nutrients*, 13(5), 1571. https://doi.org/10.3390/nu13051571.

Rowe, S. B. (2002). Communicating science-based food and nutrition information. *The Journal of Nutrition*, 132(8), 2481S–2482S. https://doi.org/10.1093/jn/132.8.2481S.

Ruben, R., Cavatassi, R., Lipper, L., Smaling, E., & Winters, P. (2021). Towards food systems transformation – Five paradigm shifts for healthy, inclusive and sustainable food systems. *Food Security*, 13(6), 1423–1430. https://doi.org/10.1007/s12571-021-01221-4.

Rust, N. A., Ridding, L., Ward, C., et al. (2020). How to transition to reduced-meat diets that benefit people and the planet. *Science of the Total Environment*, 718, 137208. https://doi.org/10.1016/j.scitotenv.2020.137208.

Rutten, M., Achterbosch, T. J., de Boer, I. J. M., et al. (2018). Metrics, models and foresight for European sustainable food and nutrition security: The vision of the SUSFANS project. *Agricultural Systems*, 163, 45–57. https://doi.org/10.1016/j.agsy.2016.10.014.

Sako, S. (2006). Challenges facing Africa's Regional Economic Communities in Capacity Building. The Institute of Development Studies and Partner Organisations. Report. https://hdl.handle.net/20.500.12413/2966

Sandhu, H. (2021). Bottom-up transformation of agriculture and food systems. *Sustainability*, 13(4), 1–13. https://doi.org/10.3390/su13042171.

Sarabia, N., Peris, J., & Segura, S. (2021). Transition to agri-food sustainability, assessing accelerators and triggers for transformation: Case study in Valencia, Spain. *Journal of Cleaner Production*, 325, 129228. https://doi.org/10.1016/j.jclepro.2021.129228.

Sargant, E. (2014). *Sustainable Food Consumption: A Practice Based Approach* (Vol. 11). Wageningen Academic. https://doi.org/10.3920/978-90-8686-811-7.

Schiller, K., Godek, W., Klerkx, L., & Poortvliet, P. M. (2020). Nicaragua's agroecological transition: Transformation or reconfiguration of the agri-food regime? *Agroecology and Sustainable Food Systems*, 44(5), 611–628. https://doi.org/10.1080/21683565.2019.1667939.

Schneider, A., Hinton, J., Collste, D., et al. (2020). Can transnational corporations leverage systemic change towards a "sustainable" future? *Nature Ecology & Evolution*, 4(4), 491–492. https://doi.org/10.1038/s41559-020-1143-4.

Schoneveld, G. C. (2022). Transforming food systems through inclusive agribusiness. *World Development*, 158, 105970. https://doi.org/10.1016/j.worlddev.2022.105970.

Schot, J., & Geels, F. W. (2007). Niches in evolutionary theories of technical change: A critical survey of the literature. *Journal of Evolutionary Economics*, 17(5), 605–622. https://doi.org/10/cn84pn.

Schot, J., & Geels, F. W. (2008). Strategic niche management and sustainable innovation journeys: Theory, findings, research agenda, and policy. *Technology Analysis & Strategic Management*, 20(5), 537–554. https://doi.org/10.1080/09537320802292651.

Schwarz, G., Vanni, F., & Miller, D. (2021). The role of transdisciplinary research in the transformation of food systems. *Agricultural and Food Economics*, 9(1), 35, s40100-021-00207-2. https://doi.org/10.1186/s40100-021-00207-2.

Sen, A. (1983). *Poverty and Famines: An Essay on Entitlement and Deprivation*. Oxford University Press. www.oxfordscholarship.com/view/10.1093/0198284632.001.0001/acprof-9780198284635.

Seta, M. H. D., Oliveira, C. V. dos S., & Pepe, V. L. E. (2017). Health protection in Brazil: The national sanitary surveillance system. *Ciência & Saúde Coletiva*, 22(10), 3225–3235. https://doi.org/10.1590/1413-812320172210.16672017.

Shangguan, S., Afshin, A., Shulkin, M., et al. (2019). A meta-analysis of food labeling effects on consumer diet behaviors and industry practices. *American Journal of Preventive Medicine*, 56(2), 300–314. https://doi.org/10.1016/j.amepre.2018.09.024.

Sharpe, B., Hodgson, A., Leicester, G., Lyon, A., & Fazey, I. (2016). Three horizons: A pathways practice for transformation. *Ecology and Society*, 21(2), 47–52. https://doi.org/10.5751/ES-08388-210247.

Shepherd, I. (2018, June 12). How Chile Took on Kinder Eggs and Tony the Tiger to Fight Obesity. EAT. https://eatforum.org/learn-and-discover/how-chile-took-on-kinder-eggs-and-tony-the-tiger-to-fight-obesity/.

Shove, E., & Pantzar, M. (2005). Consumers, producers and practices: Understanding the invention and reinvention of Nordic walking. *Journal of Consumer Culture*, 5(1), 43–64. https://doi.org/10/d3bbwt.

Shove, E., Pantzar, M., & Watson, M. (2012). *The Dynamics of Social Practice: Everyday Life and How It Changes*. Sage Publications. https://doi.org/10.4135/9781446250655.

Shove, E., & Walker, G. (2014). What is energy for? Social practice and energy demand. *Theory, Culture & Society*, 31(5), 41–58. https://doi.org/10/gf38s2.

Sibanda, L. M., & Mwamakamba, S. N. (2021). Policy considerations for African food systems: Towards the United Nations 2021 Food Systems Summit. *Sustainability*, 13(16), Article 16. https://doi.org/10.3390/su13169018.

Sidaner, E., Balaban, D., & Burlandy, L. (2013). The Brazilian school feeding programme: An example of an integrated programme in support of food and nutrition security. *Public Health Nutrition*, 16(6), 989–994. https://doi.org/10.1017/S1368980012005101.

Sievert, K., Lawrence, M., Parker, C., & Baker, P. (2021). Understanding the political challenge of red and processed meat reduction for healthy and sustainable food systems: A narrative review of the literature. *International Journal of Health Policy and Management*, 10(12), 793–808. https://doi.org/10.34172/ijhpm.2020.238.

Silvestri, C., Silvestri, L., Piccarozzi, M., & Ruggieri, A. (2024). Toward a framework for selecting indicators of measuring sustainability and circular economy in the agri-food sector: A systematic literature review. *The*

International Journal of Life Cycle Assessment, 29(8), 1446–1484. https://doi.org/10.1007/s11367-022-02032-1.

Singh, B. K., Arnold, T., Biermayr-Jenzano, P., et al. (2021). Enhancing science – Policy interfaces for food systems transformation. *Nature Food*, 2(11), 838–842.

Smith, A. (2006). Green niches in sustainable development: The case of organic food in the United Kingdom. *Environment and Planning C: Government and Policy*, 24(3), 439–458. https://doi.org/10.1068/c0514j.

Smith, L. C., & Haddad, L. (2015). Reducing child undernutrition: Past drivers and priorities for the Post-MDG era. *World Development*, 68, 180–204. https://doi.org/10.1016/j.worlddev.2014.11.014.

Sneyd, L. Q., Legwegoh, A., & Fraser, E. D. G. (2013). Food riots: Media perspectives on the causes of food protest in Africa. *Food Security*, 5(4), 485–497. https://doi.org/10.1007/s12571-013-0272-x.

Soares, P., Davó-Blanes, M. C., Martinelli, S. S., Melgarejo, L., & Cavalli, S. B. (2017). The effect of new purchase criteria on food procurement for the Brazilian school feeding program. *Appetite*, 108, 288–294. https://doi.org/10.1016/j.appet.2016.10.016.

Sodano, V., & Gorgitano, M. T. (2022). Framing political issues in food system transformative changes. *Social Sciences*, 11(10), Article 10. https://doi.org/10.3390/socsci11100459.

Sonnino, R., Tegoni, C. L. S., & De Cunto, A. (2019). The challenge of systemic food change: Insights from cities. *Cities*, 85, 110–116. https://doi.org/10.1016/j.cities.2018.08.008.

Spaargaren, G., Loeber, A. M., & Oosterveer, P. (2011). *Food Practices in Transition*. Routledge.

Statista. (2013). U.S. commercial red meat production 2022. Statista. www.statista.com/statistics/219109/us-commercial-red-meat-production-since-1990/.

Stephens, P. (2021). Social finance for sustainable food systems: Opportunities, tensions and ambiguities. *Agriculture and Human Values*, 38(4), 1123–1137. https://doi.org/10.1007/s10460-021-10222-0.

Stilgoe, J., Owen, R., & Macnaghten, P. (2013). Developing a framework for responsible innovation. *Research Policy*, 42(9), 1568–1580. https://doi.org/10.1016/j.respol.2013.05.008.

Stubbs, R. (2008). The ASEAN alternative? Ideas, institutions and the challenge to "global" governance. *The Pacific Review*, 21(4), 451–468. https://doi.org/10.1080/09512740802294713.

Stuckler, D., & Nestle, M. (2012). Big food, food systems, and global health. *PLoS Medicine*, 9(6), e1001242. https://doi.org/10.1371/journal.pmed.1001242.

Good Jobs First. (2023). Subsidy Tracker. https://subsidytracker.goodjobsfirst.org/parent/tyson-foods

Suzanne, G. (2004). Local Capacity Building in Title II Food Security Projects: A Framework. USAID. www.fantaproject.org/sites/default/files/resources/FFPOP3_Localcapacity_2004.pdf.

Swinburn, B. (2019). Power dynamics in 21st-century food systems. *Nutrients*, 11(10), 2544. https://doi.org/10.3390/nu11102544.

Swinburn, B., Kraak, V., Rutter, H., et al. (2015). Strengthening of accountability systems to create healthy food environments and reduce global obesity. *The Lancet*, 385(9986), 2534–2545. https://doi.org/10.1016/S0140-6736(14)61747-5.

Swinnen, J. (2018). Political coalitions in agricultural and food policies. In J. Swinnen (Ed.), *The Political Economy of Agricultural and Food Policies* (pp. 13–34). Palgrave Macmillan. https://doi.org/10.1057/978-1-137-50102-8_2.

Szanton, D. L. (2004). *The Politics of Knowledge: Area Studies and the Disciplines*. University of California Press.

Takeshima, H., & Liverpool-Tasie, L. S. O. (2015). Fertilizer subsidies, political influence and local food prices in sub-Saharan Africa: Evidence from Nigeria. *Food Policy*, 54, 11–24. https://doi.org/10.1016/j.foodpol.2015.04.003.

Tälle, M., Wiréhn, L., Ellström, D., et al. (2019). Synergies and trade-offs for sustainable food production in Sweden: An integrated approach. *Sustainability*, 11(3), Article 3. https://doi.org/10.3390/su11030601.

Tan, H. S. G., Fischer, A. R. H., van Trijp, H. C. M., & Stieger, M. (2016). Tasty but nasty? Exploring the role of sensory-liking and food appropriateness in the willingness to eat unusual novel foods like insects. *Food Quality and Preference*, 48, 293–302. https://doi.org/10.1016/j.foodqual.2015.11.001.

Tanrikulu, H., Neri, D., Robertson, A., & Mialon, M. (2020). Corporate political activity of the baby food industry: The example of Nestlé in the United States of America. *International Breastfeeding Journal*, 15(1), 1–12. https://doi.org/10.1186/s13006-020-00268-x.

Termeer, C. J. A. M., Drimie, S., Ingram, J., Pereira, L., & Whittingham, M. J. (2018). A diagnostic framework for food system governance arrangements: The case of South Africa. *Njas-Wageningen Journal of Life Sciences*, 84, 85–93. https://doi.org/10.1016/j.njas.2017.08.001.

The Economist. (2025). Food Sustainability Index. https://impact.economist.com/projects/foodsustainability/.

The World Bank. (2020). Agriculture Finance & Agriculture Insurance [Text/HTML]. World Bank. www.worldbank.org/en/topic/financialsector/brief/agriculture-finance.

Thernsjö, T. (2018). If You Shall Critique Something, then You Have to Create an Alternative – An Ethnographic Study of Navdanya Biodiversity Conservation Farm's Practices of Farming with Nature [Masters, Lund University]. https://lup.lub.lu.se/luur/download?func=downloadFile&recordOId=8947211&fileOId=8947212.

Thorpe, J., Guijt, J., Sprenger, T., et al. (2021). Multi Stakeholder Platforms as system change agents: A guide for assessing effectiveness (1–1 online resource (PDF, 24 pages): Illustrations). Wageningen Centre for Development Innovation. https://doi.org/10.18174/548294.

Thow, A. M., Ravuvu, A., Iese, V., et al. (2022). Regional governance for food system transformations: Learning from the pacific island region. *Sustainability*, 14(19), 12700. https://doi.org/10.3390/su141912700.

Timilsina, A. R. (2007). Getting the Policies Right: The Prioritization and Sequencing of Policies in Post-Conflict Countries. RAND Corporation. https://doi.org/10.7249/RGSD222.

Tomlinson, I. (2013). Doubling food production to feed the 9 billion: A critical perspective on a key discourse of food security in the UK. *Journal of Rural Studies*, 29, 81–90. https://doi.org/10/c6t5ss.

Torres-Salcido, G., & Sanz-Canada, J. (2018). Territorial governance: A comparative research of local agro-food systems in Mexico. *Agriculture-Basel*, 8(2), 18. https://doi.org/10.3390/agriculture8020018.

Tregear, A. (2011). Progressing knowledge in alternative and local food networks: Critical reflections and a research agenda. *Journal of Rural Studies*, 27(4), 419–430. https://doi.org/10.1016/j.jrurstud.2011.06.003.

Troise, C., Tani, M., Dinsmore, J., & Schiuma, G. (2021). Understanding the implications of equity crowdfunding on sustainability-oriented innovation and changes in agri-food systems: Insights into an open innovation approach. *Technological Forecasting and Social Change*, 171, 120959. https://doi.org/10.1016/j.techfore.2021.120959.

Tsan, M., Totapally, S., Hailu, M., & Addom, B. K. (2019). The digitalisation of African agriculture report 2018–2019: Executive summary. CTA/Dalberg Advisers. https://cgspace.cgiar.org/bitstream/handle/10568/103198/Executive%20Summary%20V4.5%20ONLINE.pdf?sequence=1&isAllowed=y.

Tschirley, D., Haggblade, S., & Reardon, T. (2014). Africa's Emerging Food System Transformation – Eastern and Southern Africa. Global Center for Food Systems Innovation (GCFSI). https://gcfsi.isp.msu.edu/files/7214/6229/3434/w1.pdf.

TSI. (2025). Technology Sustainability index (TSi). Technology Sustainability Index (TSi). https://tsi.life/.

Tsuda, M., Takahashi, K. I., Hara, M., et al. (2007). New index for social impact assessment of ICT services. *Proceedings of the 2007 IEEE International Symposium on Electronics and the Environment*, 16–18. https://doi.org/10.1109/ISEE.2007.369094.

Tui, S. H.-K., Descheemaeker, K., Valdivia, R. O., et al. (2021). Climate change impacts and adaptation for dryland farming systems in Zimbabwe: A stakeholder-driven integrated multi-model assessment. *Climatic Change*, 168(1), 10. https://doi.org/10.1007/s10584-021-03151-8.

Tummers, L. (2019). Public policy and behavior change. *Public Administration Review*, 79(6), 925–930. https://doi.org/10.1111/puar.13109.

Turnhout, E., Duncan, J., Candel, J., et al. (2021). Do we need a new science-policy interface for food systems? *Science*, 373(6559), 1093–1095. https://doi.org/10.1126/science.abj5263.

Tyfield, D., Lave, R., Randalls, S., & Thorpe, C. (2017). *The Routledge Handbook of the Political Economy of Science*. Routledge.

UN Food Systems Coordination Hub. (2024). Food Systems Transformation Review and Stocktake on the Progress of Food Systems Transformation: Progress, Challenges, and Best Practices. www.unfoodsystemshub.org/docs/unfoodsystemslibraries/regional-progress-reviews/africa/national-pathway-progress-review_unfs-coordination-hub.pdf.

USDA. (2013). Financial Year 2013: Budget Summary and Annual Performance. www.obpa.usda.gov/budsum/FY13budsum.pdf

USDA. (2025). Ag and Food Statistics: Charting the Essentials – Ag and Food Sectors and the Economy | Economic Research Service. www.ers.usda.gov/data-products/ag-and-food-statistics-charting-the-essentials/ag-and-food-sectors-and-the-economy.

Vågsholm, I., Arzoomand, N. S., & Boqvist, S. (2020). Food security, safety, and sustainability – Getting the trade-offs right. *Frontiers in Sustainable Food Systems*, 4. https://doi.org/10.3389/fsufs.2020.00016.

Val, V. (2023). To do, to know, and to be: A firsthand account of Cuban agroecology. *The Journal of Peasant Studies*, 50(3), 809–81980.

Valdivia, R. O., Antle, J. M., & Stoorvogel, J. J. (2012). Coupling the tradeoff analysis model with a market equilibrium model to analyze economic and environmental outcomes of agricultural production systems. *Agricultural Systems*, 110, 17–29. https://doi.org/10.1016/j.agsy.2012.03.003.

van Bers, C., Delaney, A., Eakin, H., et al. (2019). Advancing the research agenda on food systems governance and transformation. *Current Opinion in Environmental Sustainability*, 39, 94–102. https://doi.org/10.1016/j.cosust.2019.08.003.

Van den Berg, L., Behagel, J. H., Verschoor, G., Petersen, P., & da Silva, M. G. (2022). Between institutional reform and building popular movements: The political articulation of agroecology in Brazil. *Journal of Rural Studies*, 89, 140–148. https://doi.org/10.1016/j.jrurstud.2021.11.016.

Van Den Bold, M., Kohli, N., Gillespie, S., et al. (2015). Is there an enabling environment for nutrition-sensitive agriculture in South Asia? Stakeholder perspectives from India, Bangladesh, and Pakistan. *Food and Nutrition Bulletin*, 36(2), 231–247. https://doi.org/10/f7rrxt.

Van Gameren, V., Ruwet, C., & Bauler, T. (2015). Towards a governance of sustainable consumption transitions: How institutional factors influence emerging local food systems in Belgium. *Local Environment*, 20(8), 874–891. https://doi.org/10.1080/13549839.2013.872090.

Vanloqueren, G., & Baret, P. V. (2009). How agricultural research systems shape a technological regime that develops genetic engineering but locks out agroecological innovations. *Research Policy*, 38(6), 971–983. https://doi.org/10.1016/j.respol.2009.02.008.

Verbruggen, P. (2013). Gorillas in the closet? Public and private actors in the enforcement of transnational private regulation. *Regulation & Governance*, 7(4), 512–532. https://doi.org/10.1111/rego.12026.

Vercillo, S., Kuuire, V. Z., Armah, F. A., & Luginaah, I. (2015). Does the new alliance for food security and nutrition impose biotechnology on smallholder farmers in Africa? *Global Bioethics*, 26(1), 1–13. https://doi.org/10/ggt6d7.

Vermeir, I., Weijters, B., De Houwer, J., et al. (2020). Environmentally sustainable food consumption: A review and research agenda from a goal-directed perspective. *Frontiers in Psychology*, 11, 1–24. www.frontiersin.org/articles/10.3389/fpsyg.2020.01603.

Virmani, A., & François Lépineux. (2015). Spiritual-based entrepreneurship for an alternative food culture: The transformational power of Navdanya. In L. Zsolnai (Ed.), *The Spiritual Dimension of Business Ethics and Sustainability Management* (pp. 125–142). Springer. https://doi.org/10.1007/978-3-319-11677-8.

Von Braun, J. (2008). *Food and Financial Crises: Implications for Agriculture and the Poor*. International Food Policy Research Institute. www.dairyknowledge.in/sites/default/files/food_and_financial_crisis-_implications_for_agriculture_and_the_poor.pdf

von Braun, J. (2009). Addressing the food crisis: Governance, market functioning, and investment in public goods. *Food Security*, 1(1), 9–15. https://doi.org/10.1007/s12571-008-0001-z.

von Braun, J. (2010). Food insecurity, hunger and malnutrition: Necessary policy and technology changes. *New Biotechnology*, 27(5), 449–452. https://doi.org/10.1016/j.nbt.2010.08.006.

von Braun, J., Afsana, K., Fresco, L. O., & Hassan, M. H. A. (2023). Science for transformation of food systems: Opportunities for the UN Food Systems Summit. In J. von Braun et al. (Eds.), *Science and Innovations for Food Systems Transformation* (pp. 921–948). Springer.

von Braun, J., & Kalkuhl, M. (2015). International Science and Policy Interaction for Improved Food and Nutrition Security: Toward an International Panel on Food and Nutrition (IPFN). ZEF Working Paper Series.

Wallbaum, H., Krank, S., & Teloh, R. (2011). Prioritizing sustainability criteria in urban planning processes: Methodology application. *Journal of Urban Planning and Development*, 137(1), 20–28. https://doi.org/10.1061/(ASCE)UP.1943-5444.0000038.

Webb, P., Benton, T. G., Beddington, J., et al. (2020). The urgency of food system transformation is now irrefutable. *Nature Food*, 1(10), 584–585. https://doi.org/10.1038/s43016-020-00161-0.

Wendin, K. M., & Nyberg, M. E. (2021). Factors influencing consumer perception and acceptability of insect-based foods. *Current Opinion in Food Science*, 40, 67–71. https://doi.org/10.1016/j.cofs.2021.01.007.

Wenzel, P. (2007). Public-sector transformation in South Africa: Getting the basics right. *Progress in Development Studies*, 7(1), 47–64. https://doi.org/10.1177/146499340600700105.

White, S., Schmidt, W., Sahanggamu, D., et al. (2016). Can gossip change nutrition behaviour? Results of a mass media and community-based intervention trial in East Java, Indonesia. *Tropical Medicine & International Health*, 21(3), 348–364. https://doi.org/10.1111/tmi.12660.

Whitfield, L. (2017). New paths to capitalist agricultural production in Africa: Experiences of Ghanaian pineapple producer – Exporters. *Journal of Agrarian Change*, 17(3), 535–556. https://doi.org/10/f99qww.

WHO. (2025). Food Safety. www.who.int/news-room/fact-sheets/detail/food-safety.

Wiebe, K., & Prager, S. (2021). Commentary on foresight and trade-off analysis for agriculture and food systems. *Q Open*, 1(1), qoaa004. https://doi.org/10.1093/qopen/qoaa004.

Wilkinson, G. R., Schofield, M., & Kanowski, P. (2014). Regulating forestry – Experience with compliance and enforcement over the 25 years of Tasmania's forest practices system. *Forest Policy and Economics*, 40, 1–11. https://doi.org/10.1016/j.forpol.2013.11.010.

Wilks, M., Phillips, C. J., Fielding, K., & Hornsey, M. J. (2019). Testing potential psychological predictors of attitudes towards cultured meat. *Appetite*, 136, 137–145. https://doi.org/10.1016/j.appet.2019.01.027.

Willett, W., Rockström, J., Loken, B., et al. (2019). Food in the Anthropocene: The EAT – Lancet Commission on healthy diets from sustainable food systems. *The Lancet*, 393(10170), 447–492. https://doi.org/10.1016/S0140-6736(18)31788-4.

Willis, D. (2015, August 12). Represent. ProPublica. https://projects.propublica.org/represent/lobbying.

Winne, M. (2005). Community food security: Promoting food security and building healthy food systems. Venice: Community Food Security Coalition.

Woodhill, J. (2023, January 24). Why, What, and How: A Framework for Transforming Food Systems. Foresight4Food. https://foresight4food.net/why-what-and-how-a-framework-for-transforming-food-systems/.

World Health Organization. (2020). *The State of Food Security and Nutrition in the World 2020: Transforming Food Systems for Affordable Healthy Diets* (Vol. 2020). Food & Agriculture Org.

Wu, X., Ramesh, M., & Howlett, M. (2015). Policy capacity: A conceptual framework for understanding policy competences and capabilities. *Policy and Society*, 34(3–4), 165–171. https://doi.org/10.1016/j.polsoc.2015.09.001.

Yates, J., Gillespie, S., Savona, N., Deeney, M., & Kadiyala, S. (2021). Trust and responsibility in food systems transformation. Engaging with Big Food: Marriage or mirage? *BMJ Global Health*, 6(11), e007350. https://doi.org/10.1136/bmjgh-2021-007350.

Yee, W.-H., & Liu, P. (2021). Governance capacity and regulatory enforcement: Street-level organizations in Beijing's food safety reform. *International Review of Administrative Sciences*, 87(2), 256–274. https://doi.org/10.1177/0020852321992110.

Ying, L., & Mengqing, S. (2011). Literature Analysis of Innovation Diffusion. *Technology and Investment*, 2(3), 155–1622. doi: 10.4236/ti.2011.23016.

Zerbian, T., Adams, M., Dooris, M., & Pool, U. (2022). The role of local authorities in shaping local food systems. *Sustainability*, 14(19), 12004. https://doi.org/10.3390/su141912004.

Zerbian, T., & de Luis Romero, E. (2021). The role of cities in good governance for food security: Lessons from Madrid's urban food strategy. *Territory, Politics, Governance*, 11(4), 794–812. https://doi.org/10.1080/21622671.2021.1873174.

Zorell, C. (2019). *Varieties of Political Consumerism: From Boycotting to Buycotting*. Palgrave Macmillan. https://doi.org/10.1007/978-3-319-91047-5.

Zurek, M., Hebinck, A., Leip, A., et al. (2018). Assessing sustainable food and nutrition security of the EU food system – An integrated approach. *Sustainability*, 10(11), 4271. https://doi.org/10.3390/su10114271.

Zurek, M., Hebinck, A., & Selomane, O. (2021). Looking across diverse food system futures: Implications for climate change and the environment. *Q Open*, 1(1), qoaa001. https://doi.org/10.1093/qopen/qoaa001.

Zurek, M., Leip, A., Kuijsten, A., et al. (2017). Deliverable No. 1.3: Sustainability metrics for the EU food system: A review across economic, environmental and social considerations. Scientific Report. https://susfans.eu/system/files/public_files/Publications/Reports/SUSFANS-Deliverable-%20D1.3-UOXF.pdf

Acknowledgements

The authors declare that financial support was received for the research, authorship, and/or publication of this Element. This research was supported by the Sustainable and Healthy Diet through Food System Transformation (SHiFT) initiative funded under CGIAR.

Cambridge Elements

Sustainability: Science, Policy, Practice

Series Editor-in-Chief
Arun Agrawal
University of Michigan
Arun Agrawal is Samuel Trask Dana Professor in the School for Environment and Sustainability at the University of Michigan. His research focuses on the political economy of human–environment interactions and systems, sustainability of social ecological systems, governance of natural resources, inter-temporal and cross-scale dynamics of socio-environmental changes, and the effects of climate change on conflict and health outcomes.

Advisory Editorial Board
Neil Adger, *University of Exeter*
Anthony Bebbington, *The Ford Foundation*
Christoph Béné, *Alliance Bioversity International*
William Clark, *Harvard University*
Ruth S. DeFries, *Columbia University*
Melissa Leach, *University of Sussex*
Diana Liverman, *University of Arizona*
Yadvinder Malhi, *University of Oxford*
Debra Rowe, *Oakland Community College*
B.L. Turner II, *Arizona State University*
Esther Turnhout, *University of Twente*

Editorial Board
Vanesa Castan Broto, *The University of Sheffield*
Paul J. Ferraro, *Johns Hopkins University*
Reetika Khera, *Indian Institute of Technology Delhi*
Myanna Lahsen, *Linköping University*
Christian Lund, *University of Copenhagen*
Johan Oldekop, *University of Manchester*
Laura Vang Rasmussen, *University of Copenhagen*
Diana Ürge-Vorsatz, *Central European University*

About the Series
This series showcases scholarship that investigates persistent, multi-scale challenges to global sustainability. It facilitates the consolidation of the science and social science of sustainability, bridging the gap between knowledge, policy, and practice. It aims to include the best reviews of relevant themes related to environment, development, and sustainability.

Cambridge Elements

Sustainability: Science, Policy, Practice

Elements in the Series

Girl Power: Sustainability, Empowerment, and Justice
Jin In

Climate Change on Trial: Mobilizing Human Rights Litigation to Accelerate Climate Action
César Rodríguez-Garavito

How To Normatively Transform Food Systems: Propositions of a Holistic Framework of Politics
Abdul-Rahim Abdulai and Christophe Béné

A full series listing is available at: www.cambridge.org/ESBL

For EU product safety concerns, contact us at Calle de José Abascal, 56–1°, 28003 Madrid, Spain or eugpsr@cambridge.org.

www.ingramcontent.com/pod-product-compliance
Lightning Source LLC
LaVergne TN
LVHW010301260326
834688LV00044B/1392